UNMEASURED STRENGTH

UNMEASURED

—

STRENGTH

LAUREN MANNING

HENRY HOLT AND COMPANY   NEW YORK

Henry Holt and Company, LLC
Publishers since 1866
175 Fifth Avenue
New York, New York 10010
www.henryholt.com

Henry Holt® and 🛡® are registered trademarks of
Henry Holt and Company, LLC.

Library of Congress Cataloging-in-Publication Data
Manning, Lauren.
Unmeasured strength / Lauren Manning. — 1st ed.
    p.   cm.
ISBN 978-0-8050-9463-3
 1. Manning, Lauren.   2. September 11 Terrorist Attacks, 2001—Biography.
3. Victims of terrorism—New York (State)—New York—Biography.
4. Terrorism—New York (State)—New York—Biography.   5. Terrorism—
United States—Biography.   6. Resilience (Personality trait)   I. Title.
HV6432.7.M337 2011
974.7'1044092—dc23
[B]
                                                            2011024019

Henry Holt books are available for special promotions and
premiums. For details contact: Director, Special Markets.

First Edition 2011

Designed by Kelly S. Too

Printed in the United States of America
1   3   5   7   9   10   8   6   4   2

For Tyler, Jagger, and Greg

Your life throbs deep, but rising,
Of unmeasured strength, no power
As great to link two souls
As love
Perfectly spoken.

—GREG MANNING
(The Beach Café, New York, September 30, 2001)

CONTENTS

UNMEASURED STRENGTH

EVERYTHING MOVES

> It is better to conquer yourself than to win a thousand battles.
> Then the victory is yours. It cannot be taken from you, not by
> angels or by demons, heaven or hell.
>
> BUDDHA

I rush out of our apartment at about 8:30 a.m., annoyed to be running so late but glad, after the turmoil of the previous night, to be on my way to work.

Normally I would be out the door by 8:00 a.m., but just as I was about to leave I received a call from Mari Fitzpatrick, the caretaker at our weekend home in Pine Plains, New York. A real estate appraisal of the house is scheduled for later today, but the key for the appraiser has disappeared. Our summer renters had dropped it off earlier this morning, putting it in an envelope taped to a shopping bag that carried a freshly baked apple pie. They'd hung the bag from the knob of Mari's back door, but Maggie, Mari's free-ranging black lab, had found the pie and wolfed it down, and the key was nowhere to be found among the crumbs. Fortunately, I was able to reach Billie Woods, a friend and realtor who also has a spare key and who lives nearby in Rhinebeck, and she agreed to be there to open the house.

Now, after a kiss for my son, Tyler, a quick hello to Joyce, his babysitter, and a barely grumbled good-bye to my husband, Greg, I am finally on my way. I walk up Perry Street to Washington Street, where I wait several minutes trying to hail a cab. But soon enough I am riding south, making a right on Houston Street, then left to join the morning crush of cars and trucks inching down West Street toward the World Trade Center.

I glance at my watch, and again I'm irritated by how late it is. The watch is gold and silver, an engagement gift from Greg, and for a moment I wonder if I should have worn my silver watch instead, since it might have gone better with the slate-gray silk suit I'm wearing. Across the Hudson River, the Jersey City skyline is bright and sharp against a backdrop of dazzling, pure blue sky. The river is a deep gray, its wind-driven swells crisscrossed by the wakes of morning water taxis. I grow impatient when we are caught at yet another red light, but before long we are turning left across West Street to the carport entrance to One World Trade Center.

As the taxi pulls under the clear roof of the porte cochere, I take out my wallet to pay the driver. Two cabs in front of us pull forward, and I ask my driver to move up a bit so I can get out directly in front of the building's entrance. I step out of the cab, thinking how warm it is for September, how just the week before we were still at the beach in Bridgehampton. Heading for the revolving doors, I walk past the security barriers, which are barely camouflaged as large concrete planters. As I approach the building, I look through the glass and see two women standing and talking inside. I smile at them as I push through the revolving doors. Then I move through a second set of doors and enter the lobby, where I am jarred by an incredibly loud, piercing whistle.

I hesitate for a moment before attributing the noise to some nearby construction project and continuing toward the elevators.

Directly ahead, elevator banks serve floors 1 through 43, and a central freight elevator serves every floor from 1 through 107. To my right, two elevators on the lobby's south side go straight to Windows on the World, the restaurant on the 107th floor. These two are flanked by eight more that go to a sky lobby on the 44th floor. To my left, on the north side of the lobby, twelve express elevators serve the 78th floor sky lobby, where I will catch a second elevator to reach my 105th-floor office at Cantor Fitzgerald.

As I veer left toward my elevators, I suddenly feel an incredible sense of otherworldliness. It's an odd, tremendous, quaking feeling, and everything . . . moves. The entire 110-story tower is trembling.

Then I hear a huge, whistling rush of air, an incredibly loud sound: *shshooooooooooooooo*. My adversary is racing toward me, howling in fury at its containment as it plummets to meet me from above the 90th floor.

This is the moment and place of our introduction.

With an enormous, screeching exhalation, the fire explodes from the elevator banks into the lobby and engulfs me, its tentacles of flame hungrily latching on. An immense weight pushes down on me, and I can barely breathe. I am whipped around. Looking to my right toward where the two women were talking, I see people lying on the floor covered in flames, burning alive.

Like them, I am on fire.

God asks us to speak, to record the memories that mark our lives. This is the living testament, then, of the times and places and things I have done that mark my days on Earth.

Since 9/11, I have often been asked to share my story, but it is always with a certain awkwardness that I talk about myself or my personal feelings. I am much more comfortable telling a joke, chatting about the headline of the moment, or drawing others in by asking about their lives. Rarely will I turn the conversation in my own direction. My parents frowned on self-congratulation, and so even when my siblings and I had a right to be proud of our accomplishments, we were told to be humble. Alongside hard work, the trait my parents seemed to value the most was humility. So telling my story has its challenges.

Here is the simple version of what happened: I went to work one morning and was engulfed by the fires that would bring down the twin towers of the World Trade Center. I fled the building in flames, so terribly injured that almost no one held out any hope for me. Yet in the weeks and months that followed, I battled back from the edge of death to hold my child in my arms and intertwine my husband's fingers with what was left of my own. In almost every way, this is the story of a miracle.

I will never know how many others were gravely wounded along with me during the attacks' first moments. The places where my fellow victims stood, more than a thousand feet in the air, have disappeared forever. When the buildings collapsed, they took with them thousands of lives, among them too many of my friends and colleagues. By the smallest of margins, I was given a chance to survive, and I decided, early that morning, that I would never give up the fight to live. I would never surrender.

The tale I have to tell is full of adventure, though not in the conventional sense. I did not need to travel to the ends of the earth, scale prodigious mountains, or challenge vast oceans to find the ultimate tests of endurance. I faced death every day for almost three months, armed only with the breath in my lungs and the strength in my heart. After I emerged from weeks of darkness, I discovered that the simplest of tasks were beyond my ability, and that accomplishing them would require equal measures of defiance and will. It took months to learn to breathe on my own again, to recover the ability to speak, to relearn how to walk. It took years to recover the most basic semblance of a normal life.

I was blessed by the support and comfort provided by my loved ones, and strengthened by the belief from within that I could reclaim my life. The guardians of my heart—my husband, my son, and the rest of my family—cradled me. An enormous outpouring of letters and prayers, messages and gifts from around the world flooded our lives with a happiness that lifted me in my darkest moments, and a hope that helped fuel my survival.

Yet while I was surrounded by love, the journey through a harsh and unforgiving landscape of pain and disability was mine alone to make. That I lived, that I narrowly escaped the fate of so many others that day, is a humbling reminder of both the extreme fragility and the surprising courage that exist within all of us. What I know for certain is that there would be no story at all if I hadn't somehow held a deep faith in myself or understood the beauty and power of a simple word: *commitment*. Commitment to all that is worthwhile in life: to the people who are most important to us; to the endeavors that will yield the most good; to the acts of kindness or courage that reflect our deepest values. Commitment, I've learned, brings focus and direction, an innate sense that guides us from within, providing a compass for our lives. It also brings responsibility, most especially the requirement that we keep our word and always give our best.

Before I was injured, I had committed to any number of things. To relationships, friends, family. To hard work and a successful career. To commonplace hopes and deepest desires. Generally I had done this by relying on a quiet confidence that I could make good things happen. But the truth is, I sometimes wasn't able to do so. On occasion, I felt strangely paralyzed by the thought of achieving my goals. At other times, the effort to reach a desired destination proved so difficult that my vision of it dimmed, and eventually I moved on to new dreams.

But when 9/11 brought me to the border between life and death, and then face-to-face with monumental challenges, I understood that no matter how painful the task before me, I could not turn away. I had to make the most important commitment of all: a commitment to life itself.

It's now been a decade since that day, and sometimes I look back and wonder, *Have I accomplished anything of note or great worth?* People have called me a hero, but I can only say that I did what I needed to do. I was not the agent of my own adversity. Pain and suffering were imposed on me; they invaded and overwhelmed my body and threatened to crush my soul. Once I opened my eyes after a long climb out of the darkness, I knew that every day, I had a choice. Every day I had to fully commit to outlasting my enemies—those cowards who covered their faces from the light and screamed toward us in their metal daggers. Would I let their act of terror beat me into submission? Would I let them win? Would I let them steal my will to live, having failed to extinguish my life itself? Every day, I had to reach deep inside and find an as yet unmeasured strength that made it possible to carry on.

As I encountered and then overcame one obstacle after another, what mattered most was that I was loved. I had a husband who thought I was beautiful, even though so much of my body had been burned. I had a son who was always thrilled to see me. And luck? I had that, too. Pure luck, blind luck, and bad luck—on 9/11, I ended up with all three.

So yes, this is a story about what happened to me on September 11. But it's also about November 11, the day I first spoke again, and it's about June 11, the first time I danced again with my beautiful boy Tyler. It's about September 11, 2002, when I cheered for the glory of my lost colleagues. And it's about every day afterward.

This is the story of how I learned to live again.

1

LOOKING GLASS

The vision that you glorify in your mind, the ideal that you
enthrone in your heart, this you will build your life by, and this
you will become.

—JAMES ALLEN

When I was very young my family moved to a small village outside Frankfurt, Germany, because my father—an executive for
ITT during its heyday as an international conglomerate—had
been given a new assignment. The strange country and its
unfamiliar language fueled my eagerness for adventure, and I
often wriggled beneath the fence that surrounded our backyard
and ran off to find my friend Enga. Along with several other children in the neighborhood, we enjoyed engaging in elaborate games
of hide-and-seek. But it wasn't enough to hide from each other:
Enga and I liked to pretend that Herr Schmidt, the elderly man
who lived next door, was an evil spirit determined to do us harm.

Not far from Herr Schmidt's backyard and his neat little vegetable garden was a small roadside storage bin. One day during a
game of hide-and-seek, Enga and I pulled open the bin's hinged
front doors and clambered inside, pulling the doors closed behind

us. We were thrilled to have discovered the perfect hiding place; as time passed and none of our friends found us, we whispered excitedly that we had won the game. After a while we decided to peek out to see if anyone was still looking for us, but as we pushed on the bin's doors they wouldn't budge. In pulling the doors closed behind us, we had engaged their latch and trapped ourselves inside.

Suddenly the game was no longer fun. It was a warm day, and the air inside the bin was stifling. Crouching there in the hot darkness, we started to panic. We banged on both the locked doors and the top of the bin and yelled for help. We didn't know if anyone could hear us; our shouts seemed to stay inside the bin, the close walls reflecting our shrill cries and blasting them back at us. Worse, our screaming was soon overwhelmed by the deafening roar of a jet flying overhead on its approach to one of the nearby airports.

After waiting for the sound of the engines to fade, we resumed our shouting and banging. More time passed, but still no one came. Then we heard a second plane approach, and our voices were drowned out yet again. As the jet howled above us, Enga and I looked at each other in terrified silence, out of breath from the heat and the effort of screaming at the top of our lungs. When the noise of the second plane's engines finally faded, the silence seemed oddly amplified. All we could hear in the muffled dead air was our own breathing.

Gradually we became aware of the sound of boots crunching on gravel—someone was approaching. The footsteps got louder and then stopped. We heard a bang, and abruptly the top of the bin swung upward, bringing a flood of bright light and a rush of fresh air. A darkened figure with a pitchfork loomed above us; peering down, its face was invisible against the blazing sky. A hand groped toward the corner where the two of us cowered, now more scared than ever.

As the figure's head dipped down into the shadows, we saw who it was and felt both shock and relief. Our imagined arch-enemy, Herr Schmidt, had come to our rescue. While tending his garden, he had heard our cries for help and realized that we had locked ourselves in the bin. Miraculously, a spirit from our make-believe world of fear had saved us.

My dad, Thomas Pritchard, served in the Marines during the Korean War. After an honorable discharge he earned his degree in business and then rose through the ranks at ITT. His military bearing, baritone voice, and firm handshake commanded respect, and he left more than one teenage boyfriend of mine quaking in his sneakers.

He tolerated no laziness, physical or mental. He was extremely well read, especially in history and science. He expected you to learn not just how things worked, but what could be achieved through that understanding. He expected you to conduct your-self in all things with a sense of duty and honor. When you agreed to something, it was a contract, and he expected you to fulfill it. He expected you to get things done and get them done right.

Away from the workplace, he valued physical activity and intel-lectual curiosity. He loved maintaining his home and property. He could have paid someone else to do it, but he wanted to do it himself, and he could do it better than most. This was true whether he was building a deck, solving a plumbing problem, or wiring a new light fixture. He was a skilled golfer, and if he liked the way you hit the ball out of a particularly difficult lie, he would offer his highest praise: "That was a golf shot."

Joan, my mother, was as tough-minded, disciplined, and tire-
less as my father. She was beautiful, but at times I thought she was
made of steel: no matter what happened, she was never flustered.
She reacted to everything calmly and sensibly, and must have
had absolute confidence that she could handle whatever came her
way. She once had dreams of being a doctor, but she and my father
married when she was twenty-two, beginning a union that still
thrives almost sixty years later.

Having made the choice to be a homemaker, my mother took
care of us when we were sick, mended torn clothes, sewed cos-
tumes, played ball, and bandaged our scrapes and bruises. She
prepared homemade meals every night, and our house was always
immaculate. A capable golfer and tennis player, she was also a gifted
painter and pianist. She hosted endless dinner parties, always
trying out new recipes. Before Martha Stewart, there was Joan
Pritchard.

After our two and a half years in Germany, we moved to
Wayne, a leafy suburb in northern New Jersey. I was the eldest.
My sister, Glynis, whom we all called Gigi, was almost two years
younger, and after she came along, I wasn't very happy about sharing my parents' attention. But as we both grew older, Gigi became
my pal, at least when I wasn't in the mood to boss her around. Our
brother, Scot, six years younger than me, became our sidekick, and
until he got bigger than us, we would pick on him mercilessly.

My parents' love for their children, though rarely expressed
explicitly, was evident in the way they raised us. They considered
it their job to teach us how to be good people and good citizens,
and they believed that above all we needed to learn the value of
discipline and hard work. Both early risers, they always made sure
that everything in our home ran with clockwork precision. Every

day we were given goals or chores, something tangible that needed
to be done or studied. Each week we were given twenty words from
the dictionary, and we were required to define and use them in
sentences at the dinner table.

Though kind and generous, my parents were unyielding in
their demand that we be good students and perform extra work
beyond our assigned studies. They instilled in us the belief that
we could accomplish whatever we set out to achieve. When helping me with a school project, my mom would always tell me, "It's
going to be okay, Lauren. You'll do fine, you'll get it done." She
gave me the gift of calm confidence, and in times of turmoil it has
served me well.

My siblings and I were taught to think for ourselves and be
responsible. When I was nine, for instance, I told my father I
wanted to learn to play chess. He told me that before he would sit
down with me at a board, I had to read about each piece and
understand its actions. When I was a bit older, I told him that I
would rather mow the lawn than help my mom in the kitchen.
Fine, he said—and then he taught me how to put gas in the lawn
mower, start it up, and adjust its height. I had to learn more than
simply how to turn on the machine.

After our chores were done our mother would send us out the
door saying, "Go outside go amuse yourselves," trusting that we
would return in one piece, which for the most part we did. During the summer, Gigi and I would wander freely, told only to come
home for lunch when we heard the fire whistle at noon. As I plot-
ted adventures in our backyard and farther afield, our uncharted
time unwound like an endless spool of thread. With a group of

neighborhood kids, we explored nearby woods and searched for secret places, creating games that usually featured villains to add a sense of danger.

I was fascinated by animals, and I collected frogs, salamanders, and crayfish from a nearby stream and then brought them home to keep as pets. I also spent hours lying on the grass by the garden, sketching the blossoms or simply daydreaming in the afternoon sun. On rainy days I would curl up with a book and lose myself in its imaginary realms. Part of me secretly believed in the fantasy world of nature and animals conjured in stories like Kenneth Grahame's *The Wind in the Willows* and Frances Hodgson Burnett's *The Secret Garden*. I reread those books over and over, sketching the characters and daydreaming of magical happenings in a universe that bent to my will. I was sure that if I believed deeply enough, what I dreamed of would come true.

My parents tolerated my somewhat dreamy nature, but they also taught me that shortcuts aren't the path to achievement, and that failure is sometimes the best way to learn a difficult lesson. I recall coming home from school one day excited about the Thanksgiving play, hoping to be cast as Pocahontas. I begged my mom to practice the part with me, and she did, over and over. I felt confident when I gave my audition, but afterward my teacher said, "You did very well, Lauren, and I am pleased to say that you will play the part of an Indian squaw." She could see that I couldn't quite believe that I'd heard her right, so in front of the class she pronounced my assignment yet again.

The part of Pocahontas went to a girl named Kathy, whose hair was always perfectly set in ponytails and tied with a different color ribbon every day. She dressed in clothes that were the height of fashion, while I wore simple dresses and jumpers, many of them hand-sewn by my mother. When the day of the play came,

I stood onstage in the background, my feather slightly bent and my headband slipping down over my eyes as we sang "America the Beautiful." Nothing soothed the pain of having been rejected, but my mother—calm as always—said, "Next time, just try again."

My parents consistently encouraged me to pursue my interests, particularly in art and horseback riding. Although I excelled in both, my efforts usually seemed to fall a step short. I would participate in art competitions and in horse shows, but when I didn't come home with the blue ribbon, my instinct was to quit. Neither my mother nor my father would hear a word of it; instead, they would simply tell me to keep trying. In time, their tenacity became part of me, and all these years later I still judge myself harshly whenever I believe I haven't put forth my best effort.

Every summer our parents took us on vacations lasting three to four weeks that allowed all of us to explore and learn about the world around us. They always made sure that we had plenty of fun, but the trips—in both the United States and Europe—were also meant to be educational. My mother's job was to keep us organized and then shepherd us behind our father, who was always charging ahead to the next adventure. We practically had to chase after him as he showed us something new or choreographed a once-in-a-lifetime experience.

When I was twelve, Gigi and Scot and I traveled with my parents to Gettysburg, Pennsylvania, and stood on the ridge of Cemetery Hill. Earlier that day, we had walked the famous battlefields, past the x-frame farm fences and along the roads, tracing the lines of battle. Now, with the broad, open fields stretching before us, my dad told us stories about valor and sacrifice, and about the dangers of overconfidence. As he spoke about the bravery of the young soldiers who had fought and died in these fields, his voice occasionally broke. "You're standing where the decisive battle of the Civil War was fought," he told us. "The Union soldiers were willing to give their lives for what they believed in, and this country was saved right here."

Gazing out at the peaceful meadow, I tried to imagine the terrible battle that had taken place. I had studied the Gettysburg address and now thought of its ringing phrases, particularly those at the end: "That from these honored dead we take increased devotion to that cause for which they gave the last full measure of devotion; that we here highly resolve that these dead shall not have died in vain; that this nation, under God, shall have a new birth of freedom; and that government of the people, by the people, for the people, shall not perish from the earth."

Standing on Cemetery Hill, my father told us: "That is what it means to accept the honor of being an American. That is what it means to give honor and duty to a cause."

Until I became a teenager, I was a classic tomboy. I loved riding bikes at high speeds and digging under fences to gain access to forbidden territory. On Halloween, I dressed up as a hobo or pirate, never a princess. When I became older and more daring, my friends and I sometimes broke into school classrooms over the weekend and climbed onto the school's broad, flat roof, until we were chased away by the police. Despite my mother's continual prodding, I never cared to tuck in my shirt or to comb my hair more than once a day. Like many girls my age, I had Barbie and Ken dolls along with Pepper, Barbie's sidekick, and Pepper's nameless boyfriend. But my Barbie had one case for her accessories, just a couple of outfits, and she spent a lot of time riding my Breyer horses or climbing trees.

My time as tomboy came to an end when I was about fourteen. Childlike yearning for an imaginary world faded, replaced by the awkward self-consciousness of adolescence. I remember telling my mother, "I don't need or want a purse—I have nothing to put in it. And why is this training bra making it hard for me to breathe?" Nonplussed, my mother said, "You'll use the purse, and you'll get used to the bra."

Once I got my first issues of *Seventeen* and *Glamour*, my habits changed dramatically. Rather than rushing outside to play as soon as I got home from school, I would flip through those mesmerizing magazines and reread them until the pages became worn. I envisioned myself as one of the long-haired young women featured in the photographs, wearing iridescent eye shadow and sporting a pouty smile. I began scouting the Estée Lauder makeup counter at Stern's, a local department store. Finally I resolved to return and buy the little jar of sea-green mist eye shadow that sat nestled in the lower left corner of the glass case.

One afternoon my mom had some food shopping to do, so I asked her to drop me off at Stern's. I was dressed in a classic 1970s uniform: a blouse of white polyester crepe dotted with small green flowers, brown corduroy Levi's, and a pair of light brown Wallabees. As I walked inside, I breathed a sigh of relief—the smell of department stores had the peculiar effect of relaxing me. I approached the counter and with carefully rehearsed nonchalance pointed to the coveted jar of eye shadow. Once I'd paid for it, the salesperson smiled as she handed me the shopping bag. I don't think I fooled her one bit. She knew this was my first time buying makeup.

As soon as I got home I went straight to the bathroom—that favorite teenage hangout—and shut the door. My hands trembled as I removed the small glass jar from its box and unscrewed the top. After carefully dipping my finger in the eye shadow, I passed it over each lid. The effect was startling: my dark blue eyes were now punctuated with silver-flecked green. Drawing back to take a better look in the mirror, it occurred to me that the two stripes above my eyes made me look a bit like a tribal warrior, so I opened the medicine cabinet and dabbed some Vaseline on my lips. Puckering my mouth, I looked in the mirror again and decided that, yes, I did look at least a little more like those young women in the beauty magazines.

I walked out and proudly took a seat at the dinner table. No one in my family said a word about the "green teen" that night, not even my seven-year-old brother. Perhaps my makeover had rendered them speechless—or maybe they were all willing to give me a little space to grow into myself.

Untroubled childhood gradually yielded to the harsher reality of emerging adulthood, and my teenage years were filled with periodic rebellion, experimentation, and first love. Books became even more important to me, and my treasured stereo spun nonstop. I listened to countless hours of music from my favorite artists, and only my parents' gift of headphones permitted all of us to coexist in the same house.

Like most of my peers, I reserved my most biting criticism for my looks. Gazing at my face in the mirror, I found fault with every feature, and as my body changed, I liked almost nothing about it. For most of my teenage years, I always wore clothing that covered my arms and legs. I never wore anything backless because I didn't think I looked good.

I remember the first time I believed I might be pretty. I was eighteen; sitting on my bed looking into a small handheld mirror, I saw a young woman looking back at me with strawberry blond hair, full lips, a dimpled chin, and serious blue eyes. Something clicked, and in a rare moment of objectivity I saw that although my face hardly conformed to the golden ratio, I didn't look half bad. But once this moment of recognition passed, I returned to fretting over my appearance. Like many women, I suppose, I never quite shook that gnawing sense that I could always look better.

Though being female—let alone a decent-looking female—would prove both an asset and a burden in my professional life, both my upbringing and my days as a tomboy would ultimately serve me well. By the time I graduated from college with a BA in economics, I had come to share my parents' fervent belief in the importance of hard work, and I also knew that I wanted to work on Wall Street. In 1985, I joined the Lehman Brothers training program and went to work in its Private Client Group at 660 Madison Avenue, led by the legendary Marty Shafiroff. I earned a relatively modest salary my first year—$16,000—but I was hooked.

I loved the financial services business right from the start. Working in capital markets meant that I was involved in strengthening the underpinning of our entire economy. I wasn't just shuffling paper; I was helping create and generate transactions that would build corporations, fund new businesses, finance the construction of transit systems, and support public and private research.

Working at the nexus of the country's debt-trading machinery, I was doing my part to provide the financing that fueled the growth and prosperity of our nation. This was capitalism at its purest, and though it might sound hokey to others, it happened to be true. To me it seemed as if I had found my way to the center of the universe.

The trading floors were literal pits surrounded by rings of desks. When major economic data came out—whether the Gross National Product, the Consumer Price Index, or any key indicator of economic performance—trading would instantly surge as brokers and traders transacted millions of dollars in a frenzy of hand signals and shouted nicknames. Like so many others in my business, I found it spine-tingling to witness the intense drama of billions of dollars being turned over in just a couple of minutes.

Success was driven entirely by results. You were judged by the business you brought in and the amount of revenue you generated. But when the year came to an end, the slate was wiped clean. No matter how good you were yesterday, you had to prove yourself again today. It was a continuous and very competitive battle, everyone fighting to take, build, or enlarge a fiefdom. And the push to grow your bottom line never stopped. When the end of the day came in New York, the action would roll to Tokyo, then to London, and back to Wall Street the next morning.

As my career blossomed in the 1980s, so did my personal life. A serial monogamist, I had moved from one boyfriend to another through the years; then, after one near-engagement, I met a tall, handsome man named Kenneth DeMille Butler. Steady and hard-working, Ken dressed well and had a sharp sense of humor.

We dated for three years, and one beautiful night in October of 1989 he took me to dinner at the Plaza Hotel. In the hotel's elegant Edwardian Room, with "Moon River" playing softly in the background, Ken got down on one knee and asked me to be his wife. I said yes, and afterward, as we meandered down Fifth Avenue, I couldn't stop gazing at the sparkling jewel on my hand. As we passed Tiffany's I felt as if I had turned into Holly Golightly. The night felt like a dream plucked from one of my childhood storybooks; giddy with delight, I thought, *This is the beginning of my charmed life.*

In the life I had scripted for myself, my marriage would be a modern variation of my parents'. Like my mother and father, Ken and I would be partners in the all-important work of raising our children, but unlike my parents we would be economic equals as well. We would both have successful careers, and we would also share the household chores. Being a full-time homemaker may have been the zenith of female achievement for my mother and her generation, but not for me or mine.

My father had been the hard-charging executive, my mother the homemaker and ideal wife. She seemed to love being a full-time mother. As a teenager and burgeoning feminist, I made sure to punish her for it. At a time when more women than ever before were entering the workforce and building careers, I couldn't understand why she wasn't out working and helping the family financially. Sometimes I would confront her and ask why she didn't have a career, but she would inevitably meet my challenge with a calm rejoinder. "You just wait until you have your own marriage and your own family, then you'll realize what is best for you."

In one respect, though, I was certain that my marriage would be precisely the same as my parents'. My mother and father had been married for over thirty years by then, but they simply never fought. My siblings and I heard occasional terse words, but not a bit of real arguing. Our parents moved through the day in continuous, quiet contact, and always seemed content in each other's presence. I counted on having that sort of relationship as well. I would be my husband's peer, but I would also be the ideal wife. I saw no reason why my new husband and I couldn't be perfect partners.

After the wedding Ken and I settled into a lovely apartment with a terrace, a view, and a marble bath. It seemed like exactly the right start to our lives together, yet as the novelty of married life wore off and we settled into a routine, I began to feel a low-grade anxiety. Instead of excitement I felt an ever-present and mystifying sadness. Life did not feel charmed at all. Though outwardly everything looked perfect, inside it just didn't feel right.

Was it the apartment? For a while I thought so, and before long we moved to a new one, trading the view and the terrace for a second marble bath. But when the unhappiness followed, I decided that perhaps the city wasn't the right place for us to build a family. Why not a house in the suburbs? Surely that would do the trick.

After some months of searching, we ultimately chose a sweet little colonial set amid the towering oaks and maples of Riverside, a charming neighborhood in Greenwich, Connecticut. We could walk to the train. Our neighbors welcomed us with a basket of delicious treats. Everything oozed domesticity and comfort. But unhappiness still shadowed me, and by then I was battling a bizarre stomach demon. At least once a week, my stomach would begin heaving and then attempt to destroy itself. The ritual began as an ache and quickly built to a crescendo of doubled-over pain. These attacks always lasted about two hours, and afterward it would hurt just to inhale.

Each time the demon came I broke into a cold sweat and somehow rode it out. But one day I found myself in a concourse of the mall at the World Trade Center, doubled over and vomiting. I staggered to a Chase Bank branch, where I asked someone to call a young woman who worked for me. She came downstairs and helped me get safely to Lenox Hill Hospital; by the time I arrived, I was thinking, *This is it, I am dying.* But the doctor couldn't find anything seriously wrong with me.

This frightening episode led me to believe that I had contracted an undetectable disease or a new strain of life-threatening virus. It simply didn't occur to me that my emotions, not a physical malfunction, might be the cause of my mysterious ailment. And now I was haunted by a nightmarish scenario: I imagined a day when an attack would leave me sprawled across a hallway at work, with people walking by and gaping at me as they rushed back to the trading floor.

By 1996 I knew I was in crisis, but I couldn't see or admit its cause: the deep connection I'd believed I had with my husband simply wasn't there. A master of reattribution, I ascribed my despondency to my inadequacies as a wife rather than to my unhappy marriage. I was sure that if I could only become a better partner, my life with Ken could still improve. Continuing its assault, my body waited for my mind to catch on.

Though we had always been close, Gigi and I were very different. She was reticent; I breezily shared an endless fount of information and opinions. We often disagreed on frivolous things. In sisterly fashion, I would chide her for being perpetually late. She would sigh and say, "Lauren, you may think otherwise, but your advice isn't always right." Back and forth we'd go, relentless in our willingness to enumerate each other's faults. But we were never mean to each other.

As adults, however, we had drawn a border around one area of our lives: neither of us would discuss our failings in love. An impenetrable wall would rise at precisely the moment when we found ourselves on the brink of achieving a much deeper and more meaningful understanding. But by this point in my life, my domineering nature had mellowed a bit, and recently I had realized that her ability to see the truth was sometimes clearer than my own.

One Saturday early in the summer of 1997, Gigi came up to Greenwich for a visit. That afternoon, as we walked down our tree-lined street, we passed a neighbor's front lawn crowded with children. The husband and wife were playing a pickup game of soccer with their kids. They were all laughing and shouting to one another as they chased the ball. Seeing us, the man waved and called out, "Do you two want to join us?"

"No thanks," I said, "we can't right now. Have fun!"

It was a small moment, but somehow it seemed significant. Why was I always rushing toward or away from something but never embracing the here and now? I seemed to have no ability to be content, to simply engage in the moment. And now my marriage was disintegrating and the rigid choreography of my life was falling away. After years of denial, I had finally begun to realize how desperately unhappy I'd become; for the first time, I saw that my life would not follow the perfect trajectory I'd imagined.

At last I was ready to speak candidly with my sister about my marriage.

"Gigi, why is this happening? Every day, I wake up sad and exhausted. I take an Actifed every night just to fall asleep."

"Your body is telling you something that maybe your mind can't right now."

"It was all supposed to be so perfect; our married life would be everything we wanted."

As we continued walking, I poured my heart out and Gigi listened. A while later, we reached Tod's Point, a peninsula in Old Greenwich that juts out into Long Island Sound. We skipped rocks and looked south across the shimmering water to the north shore of the island.

"It looks so close," I said. "You could almost reach out over the water and touch it."

The summer haze had created an optical illusion, and I couldn't help but think that I'd been living with another sort of illusion. For years, I'd believed that happiness was something concrete that I could capture with my bare hands.

Gigi listened to me for hours as I began to reckon with my true feelings. Unfairly, I had always believed that I was the strong one, that my choices were somehow better than hers. But where I had been judgmental, Gigi had let me be myself. Now, as I tried to express my profound sadness, she was once again accepting me when it mattered.

As we walked back, I turned to her and said, "Sometimes, it just doesn't turn out the way we think it should, does it?"

"It's not always perfect," Gigi replied, "but you don't have to be, either."

Soon after that wrenching conversation with Gigi, Ken and I separated. I continued living in our home, but after having made such a deep commitment to another person only to see our marriage fail, the house brought me no pleasure. Instead, I threw myself into my work with even more energy and dedication than usual. My job had always been my refuge, and now it mattered more than ever.

Four years earlier, in 1993, I had made a major professional move and joined Cantor Fitzgerald, one of the world's leading bond brokerage and trading firms. My job was to run and expand the company's business development efforts, and I loved every minute of it. Then, at the start of 1996, Cantor's CEO, Howard Lutnick, asked me if I would consider going to Market Data Corporation, a company that had been spun off from Cantor Fitzgerald in the late 1980s, to market its brokerage data. Howard told me that MDC needed someone to rebuild and run the global sales force, and after he explained why he thought I'd be perfect for the job, I agreed to make the move. Soon I began working out of two offices, one on the thirty-second floor of One World Trade Center and the other at MDC's headquarters in Rye Brook in Westchester.

Unfortunately, I was walking into a difficult situation. A few months earlier, there had been an ugly falling-out between the executives of MDC and Cantor Fitzgerald. Now, as someone who had just crossed over from the enemy camp, I often felt that I'd been caught on the wrong side of the wall. The top people at MDC did not make me feel welcome, and several of their decisions undermined my opportunity to be successful. In particular, I worked for several months to market and sell a big new software product that was supposedly ready to be launched, only to learn in the end that the company wouldn't even offer it. By the summer of 1997, relations between the two companies had become so poisonous that both sides ended up in court.

That summer brought yet more change for me, both professionally and personally. Howard was well aware of how bad the situation at MDC had become, and he asked me to return to Cantor and build an internal information business that would become the successor to MDC. After a difficult year and a half, returning to my old company and settling into a new office on the 105th floor of Tower One felt like coming home.

I also made another move: now separated, I decided to rent out my house in Connecticut and move to Greenwich Village in Manhattan, trading one Greenwich for another. With Gigi's help, I found a loft apartment in the Archive, which was essentially a professional dormitory for Wall Streeters that featured a five-minute commute by taxi.

As I was settling in, my mom and dad came by and brought me some housewarming gifts, most especially a teapot. An avid tea drinker, my mom was fond of saying, "It's always good for what ails you." At that moment, it sounded like excellent advice, and before long I found myself drinking a lot of tea. The previous months had been filled with a rush of major changes: divorce, a new job, a new home. I felt as if successive waves had swept away every anchor of stability in my life. But now I was through it; I'd finally reached calmer waters. I had a new apartment and a new job with a firm I believed in and trusted. There would be no ceiling on my success.

For company I had my adopted stray cat, Caitlin, who was old and ailing but still a darling. With Caitlin purring beside me, I would sit on my couch drinking tea and imagine the road ahead. Just when many of my friends were settling down and starting families, I was completely reinventing my life. I had long since come to understand that adversity is a great teacher, and now I believed that it was time to put the lessons I'd learned to good use. It was time to find a new way forward.

2

THREE LITTLE BIRDS

Nobody has ever measured, not even poets, how much the heart can hold.

—ZELDA FITZGERALD

You never know when or where you'll meet the love of your life, but in my case it happened during a party at Windows on the World, the spectacular restaurant on the top two floors of Tower One in the World Trade Center. In late 1995, not long before I joined MDC, I attended Cantor Fitzgerald's year-end Government Securities Brokerage bash, a crowded, celebratory affair held in a banquet room on the 106th floor, one story above Cantor's main brokerage floor. The 106th and 107th floors had higher ceilings and windows that were twice as wide as those on the floors below, so the view was far more expansive and dramatic, especially at night. Looking down from that aerie, I marveled at the beauty this lent to the brilliantly lit city spread out before me, with the shoreline of New Jersey glimmering across the Hudson River.

Everyone was pleased to be ending the year on a positive note. The mood grew even more lively as the evening wore on, and at one point, I fell into an animated conversation with Dave Kravette, who had joined Cantor after running sales for MDC. A few days earlier, others at Cantor had asked me what I thought of a live market commentary product that MDC planned to introduce in the new year, in partnership with Cantor. I had not been impressed by it, and now I was sharing my concerns with Dave. When a clean-cut guy in a dark suit walked by, Dave spotted him and said, "Hey, Greg, come over here; I want to introduce you to Lauren Butler." The man turned toward us, and Dave said, "Lauren Butler, Greg Manning."

Greg reached out to shake my hand and said, "Nice to meet you."

I knew Greg's name—we had spoken on the phone a few times—but I had never laid eyes on him. He ran marketing at MDC and would be responsible for launching the live commentary service.

"Lauren doesn't like your new product," Dave said bluntly.

Wall Street has never been known to favor polite small talk, and clearly this conversation would be no exception. But Dave grinned as he delivered the line, no doubt because he and Greg had worked together for years.

Greg turned to me; he too was smiling. "Really, what don't you like about it?"

Briefly, I made the same points I'd just made during my conversation with Dave.

"I respectfully disagree," Greg said when I finished. "I think it has great potential."

But his defense of the product was hardly enthusiastic, and I immediately sensed that he shared at least some of the same concerns.

Greg quickly changed the subject, and for a few minutes we continued talking shop. Before long, though, I turned the conversation toward him and soon discovered that he played bass and loved to ski; I also learned that his first job had been at the World Trade Center.

"I liked working here," he said. "The sunsets were beautiful, and I never got seasick."

We laughed; the towers were known for swaying in high winds, and on the highest floors some people actually did get motion sickness. By then Dave had drifted away, and as my conversation with Greg continued, we stood next to a bank of windows and gazed at the city below. With the expanded perspective, Manhattan looked like a collection of flat rooftops with the downtown and uptown skylines rising out of them. The bridges resembled scale models, and the cars crossing them seemed like toys with tiny headlights.

At some point I paused and said, "Everything seems so ordered and in its place from here."

"Looking at the city from this height, you don't see the mess," Greg said. "You just see the beauty."

"I like it that way," I said.

"To beauty," Greg said, raising his glass. A few moments later, we separated and I wandered back into the crowd.

After I moved to MDC in early 1996, Greg and I worked closely on a number of projects, sometimes in agreement, sometimes in opposition. I remember having frequent discussions with him about timetables and gradually coming to understand that for him time was marvelously elastic. But since our deadlines were real, this meant that we usually found ourselves working on a project right up until the last minute. His work was consistently top notch, but getting there was always suspenseful.

By the summer of 1997, Greg, like me, had concluded that MDC's future was not particularly bright. As it happened, he left the company the same week I did, so just as I was returning to Cantor Fitzgerald, he was settling into a position as a senior vice president at Euro Brokers, a brokerage house that had its offices on the eighty-fourth floor of Tower Two. After a year and a half of working together, we would now be direct competitors.

During our time together at MDC, I had gotten to know Greg quite well. Though his manner could be a bit distant, something intriguing lurked beneath that cool surface. As I'd learned more about him, it struck me that he was a bit of a renaissance man. By day, he was a financial executive, but by night he was a bassist in a rock band.

Now Greg was happy to be working in the city again, not least because after several years of commuting to Westchester from his apartment on Perry Street in Greenwich Village, he could now reach his office in a matter of minutes. In the meantime, I had begun to explore my new neighborhood, and one Saturday I wandered into McNulty's, a coffee and tea shop near Bleecker Street that dates back to 1895. The wide-planked wood floor was lined with bins and sacks of coffee, the shelves were lined with jars of tea, and the air in the shop was saturated with a wonderful aroma.

While backing up to look at an upper shelf, I tripped on the wooden floor and stumbled backward toward a coffee barrel. Someone caught one of my arms.

"You're welcome," said a voice as I regained my footing.

Turning, I saw that it was Greg. "Thanks," I said.

I was not entirely surprised to see him. I knew he lived in the neighborhood, and in fact he had called me the day before and suggested that we share a cab to work in the morning.

"I left a message for you," Greg said. "You didn't call me back."

"I was going to," I said. "I've been busy."

Once again I noticed how handsome he was, and this time I felt an undeniable twinge of attraction. I liked his confident manner, and his eyes were a soft amber, his lips were plush, and his cheekbones were high and sculpted.

"Sure you were," he said.

We laughed and began chatting. Before we parted, we agreed to meet on Monday morning at the Archive and share a cab to work.

The taxi ride that Monday morning was so enjoyable that we made plans to take a cab home in the evening. During that second ride, Greg asked me out on a date. We had attended a number of business dinners together while working at MDC, but this promised to be a completely different sort of evening.

Several nights later, we went to the Bitter End, a club on Bleecker Street's music row. It wasn't fancy, but Greg's band, the Rolling Bones—a jam band that mostly played Rolling Stones covers—had appeared there in the past, and friends of his were up onstage that evening. The place was dark, smoky, and very loud; I felt like I was back in college, but I enjoyed the music and the club's wonderful energy.

I spent the evening watching the show, but I was well aware that Greg was spending most of his time looking at me. Before long our business relationship had fallen completely away, and it quickly became clear to me that I could really like this guy. He had always seemed so reserved, but now I understood that that was merely his professional presentation. After hours, freed from office etiquette, he had the heart of a rocker.

As we shouted over the music, Greg told me several funny stories about New York's music scene, including one about the green room at the back of the Bitter End where every band for years had signed their names on the wall.

Late in the evening, after finishing another story, Greg leaned close and said, "All that is in the front of my mind, Lauren. But now I really want to do what's been in the back of my mind."

"What's that?" I asked.

For a moment he looked into my eyes, and then he embraced me and kissed me deeply. I was dizzy with pleasure; I felt myself lifted, truly happy. This was much more than a simple kiss—I felt like we were at the center of the world.

I had never thought of myself as a person who fell head over heels in love, but this time it was different. I responded to Greg in a deep, almost visceral, way, and from the first I felt a level of comfort and honesty with him I had never experienced before. We quickly became inseparable. We saw or spoke to each other every day, and we spent a lot of time talking about and sharing our interests, whether music, sports, or bike riding. But because we worked for competitive companies, we couldn't and didn't talk about business.

The first time I visited Greg's apartment on Perry Street, he opened the door and said, "I haven't done a thing with it."

That was an understatement. The rooms were filled with a mishmash of wrought iron, antiqued wood, and hand-me-down furniture. The walls and the carpet seemed to be a continuous wrapper of indeterminate gray. For Greg, decorating was clearly not a high priority.

"Wow," I said, "this is quite a place."

"Thanks," he said with a dismissive grin.

I walked to the terrace. His apartment was so close to the water that I felt as if I were standing at the rail of a ship cruising the Hudson. "The view is sure nice."

"That's the reason I bought this place—it's all about the view."

A moment later, Greg took me in his arms and kissed me. For what seemed like the first time in years, I felt relaxed and happy. The sadness that had haunted me for so long disappeared in his embrace.

In February 1998 Greg purchased the apartment next door to his, and I moved in soon afterward. Each night we walked thirty feet from his original one-bedroom apartment containing our living room, kitchen, and study, to the new one-bedroom apartment where we had our master bedroom, and where the kitchen, stripped of its appliances, served as a makeshift walk-in closet. So technically, we weren't living together; technically, we were still neighbors.

Since the building was a co-op, Greg needed approval from the co-op's board before we could combine the two apartments. Getting the board's consent proved to be a tedious process, but when it finally came through we immediately had a door cut into the common wall separating our living room from our bedroom. As soon as it was done, Greg ceremoniously carried me over the new threshold.

Not long after this first, makeshift effort to combine the two apartments, we arranged to have dinner with my mother and father at a local French brasserie named Waterloo. It would be a big night: I was introducing Greg to my parents for the first time, and I was excited and hopeful that everyone would hit it off. But while I was getting ready to go out, I slipped on a puddle of water in our living room and fell flat on my back. Looking up, I saw a great bubbling mass in the ceiling directly above me, and a number of other water stains made it obvious that the apartment above us had flooded. We immediately alerted the building's superintendent, who discovered that a toilet gasket had failed. But the damage had been done, and it would be hours before the slow rain in our apartment stopped.

We set up pots and buckets in the living room and kitchen where the water was dripping, and then spread all the towels we owned over the rest of the floor. The buckets were filling up pretty quickly, though, so we decided to meet my mom and dad at Waterloo, and Greg would scoot back home to empty the buckets as needed.

The wine and laughter flowed at the aptly named Waterloo, as did the obstinate leak in our apartment. About every half hour, Greg had to excuse himself and go empty the buckets, but he was charming and witty in between trips home. My mom and dad both said they liked him, and we laughed when we realized that he had lived up to the old Wall Street adage for successful speeches: be funny, be short, and be gone.

Repairing a leaky apartment proved to be simple compared to the next challenge we faced. During a vacation in Saint Lucia, Greg experienced hearing loss in his left ear. He thought he'd damaged an eardrum while scuba diving, but his doctor sent him to get an MRI, and when they reviewed the results Greg learned that he had an acoustic neuroma, a glitch in the balance nerve that causes a tumor to sprout in the ear canal. He was reassured to learn that the tumor was almost certainly benign, and when he left the doctor's office he hoped that having it removed would be an unpleasant but routine procedure on par with having a root canal.

But a little later, when his doctor referred him to several neurosurgeons, Greg's expectations changed. During a visit with the first of those surgeons, Greg and I asked repeatedly about non-invasive options, but the surgeon finally cut us off and said, almost impatiently, "Listen, this is a big operation. You have a tumor next to your brain. It's the size of a golf ball, and it has to come out." We also learned that not until the tumor was removed and tested would the doctors be able to confirm that it wasn't cancerous.

To perform the operation, surgeons would drill through the skull, circle to the inner side of the ear canal, and use microsurgical knives the size of a pin to remove the tumor. The surgery carried risks of stroke, injury to the cerebellum or temporal lobe, spinal fluid leakage, meningitis, long-term balance problems, and facial paralysis. Forty years earlier the mortality rate had been 30 percent. Since then the mortality rate had plummeted, but deafness in the affected ear was virtually guaranteed.

Greg and I felt as if we'd been punched. The news had instantly drawn a line of demarcation between "before" and "after."

I ran my hand over Greg's cheek, looked into his eyes, and said, "It's going to be all right, honey; everything is going to be okay."

I wanted to take care of him, and I also decided right then that we needed to get away. I was sure that Greg would appreciate a reprieve from the anxiety building inside him. Though he wasn't showing fear and seemed calm about the prospect of the surgery, I knew his insides were churning. A dear friend of ours had been battling a malignant tumor for the previous nine months, and while Greg's odds of recovering were vastly more favorable, that didn't detract from the gravity of the situation. Brain surgery was—well, brain surgery.

Later that day, after doing a little research, I booked a weekend at the Sound View Inn on the north shore of Long Island. Claiming to be the North Fork's "Premier Resort Hotel," the inn seemed like the perfect choice. With a pool, a sauna, and a good restaurant, it would provide us with luxurious accommodations and the chance for a needed break.

A few days later, we arrived at the Sound View Inn only to discover that it was a one-story motel faced with fieldstone. Gray decking and a white porch ran the length of the inn along the waterside, but our room was a symphony of garish dissonance: the walls were an institutional bright yellow, the bedspread was a faded blue-and-white print covered with polyester pilling, and the furniture sported a shiny brown veneer. Lingering in the air was the aroma of decades of sea air mixed with the residue of thirty years of cleaning products.

When the luggage stand broke under our small duffel bag, we could only laugh.

"Maybe I should have booked the deluxe superior room," I said.

"What, and get an extra pillow?" Greg replied.

Pulling back the curtains, we sighed with relief. The view of the Sound was gorgeous.

"At least the view is as advertised," I said.

"We'll just focus on looking out, not in," Greg said.

We spent the rest of the day biking through the nearby villages and vineyards. In the early evening, we walked the beach holding hands, talking quietly about the surgery and telling each other that everything would be all right. The next day, while gazing out at the placid Sound and watching children playing on the pebbled beach, Greg made a conscious effort to push away negative thoughts and any notion that he was looking at this scene for the final time.

"This won't be the last time," he said. "We'll be coming back."

I leaned my head on his shoulder and said, "I'm looking forward to it, but next time you pick the hotel."

The night before Greg's operation, we went out to our favorite restaurant, Philip Marie. For intimate dinners, it featured a small downstairs wine cellar, with just enough room for a single table. John, the owner and chef, would offer several special items off the menu and then take your order personally.

Greg had booked this special room because it would be our last date for a while. We would begin the evening with a champagne toast to Greg's good luck—or so I thought. John brought in two flutes and poured the champagne. Then, as John passed me my glass, something dropped out of his hand into the champagne.

I was taken aback, but then I looked more closely at the glass: lying at the bottom was what appeared to be a diamond ring. Seeing the ring there, Greg seemed almost as surprised as I was, no doubt because he had expected the ring to be brought in set on a neatly folded napkin atop an elegant plate.

The ring, however, remained at the bottom of the champagne glass, and it needed to be extracted. By this point Greg and I were both laughing, because the ring itself had already popped the question. Undaunted, he retrieved the ring, wiped it dry, and in that very small room got down on one knee.

"Lauren, will you marry me?"

"Yes," I replied instantly. "I can't imagine spending my life with anyone else but you."

Greg slipped the ring on my finger, and now, suddenly, we were toasting our engagement.

The dinner was delicious, the evening full of laughter and love. Later, as we turned onto Perry Street, I said to Greg, "You'll do great tomorrow."

"Of course I will. I'm the luckiest guy in the world."

I squeezed his hand in response, and we walked a few steps in silence. Then Greg said, "Don't worry, I'll pull through."

Whatever the new day brought, we were certain of only one thing: we wanted to confront it together.

At six o'clock the next morning, we drove to New York-Presbyterian Hospital/Columbia University Medical Center. Greg's parents, Liz and Bert, joined us, and we all waited with Greg, who sat patiently with an IV in his arm. When the time for his surgery came, Greg stood up, and I kissed him gently on the lips. I tried to gather all my strength and pour it into his being with that kiss. Then, with the anesthesiologist beside him, he turned and walked down the hall, pushing the rolling IV stand toward our future.

Twelve long hours later we greeted him in the recovery room. He was experiencing a raging vertigo, feeling as if he would fly off the gurney and crash through the floor if he moved so much as a finger. The following day he projectile-vomited all over his doctor when he came to check on him, a fine thank-you for work well done. The important thing, though, was that his doctor told us that the operation had been a complete success. Greg had indeed lost most of the hearing in his left ear, and he experienced a very slight deficit in animation on the left side of his face, but fortunately he had avoided facial paralysis.

Over the next few days, physical therapists helped teach him how to walk and climb stairs again, and before the week was out he returned home with an impressive zipper of twenty-five staples down the left side of his neck. He would have to tolerate impaired balance for several months, but the tumor the surgeons had removed proved to be benign.

Greg went back to work seven weeks later. During his recovery,

I sometimes thought about the marriage vows we would soon exchange, particularly those simple and beautiful words *for better and for worse, in sickness and in health.* Neither of us had any idea how intensely we would live those words.

Once Greg was well again, we resumed planning our future. We enjoyed discussing the sort of wedding we would have. Should it be a destination weekend? Should it be in the country or the city? Should it be held on a Saturday night (as my first had been) or a Sunday afternoon (as his first had been)?

We had known from the beginning of our relationship that we wanted children, and we also agreed that we wanted two or perhaps three kids. We began trying to get pregnant immediately, but when several months went by with no results, I began thinking that I had started too late, or that I was being punished for some long-ago sin. Finally my obstetrician told us that we should consider more aggressive steps. And so we did.

We felt both excited and anxious as we entered the wood-paneled waiting room of the NYU Fertility Center, where we took our place on the red velvet chairs and couches among the other anxious couples. Men sat splay-legged in polished black tasseled loafers beside their wives. Waiting with us was a woman in traditional Muslim garb, a young Orthodox Jewish couple, a woman who appeared to be no more than twenty with what looked like a friend or sister. I wore a black suit, while Greg was dressed in navy blue pinstripes and a silk tie sprinkled with rabbits, our fertility amulet.

This group of committed, hopeful would-be parents became familiar faces as we rotated through the appointments, the blood tests, the ultrasounds, the medications, and then more blood tests

and ultrasounds. The lab-testing room was a blur of early morning activity as nervous women willed their bodies to have the
right FSH levels and their ovaries to produce enough viable and
mature eggs for retrieval.

In our refrigerator at home, boxes of Gonadotropin and other
drugs pushed aside the milk and the eggs. Greg gave me daily intra-
muscular injections of various medications. Several times each
week, especially as a retrieval loomed, I would grab a cab early in
the winter-darkened mornings for the trip to NYU to have my levels checked. Women would rush the elevator trying to get a prime
spot on the morning sign-in sheet. The afternoon was an anxious
time as I waited for a nurse to call and tell me whether my levels
were good or if we needed to adjust the level of medication. The
nurses were virtual chefs, tweaking as we went along to create the
ideal combination of ingredients.

When my hormone levels were finally right, we proceeded
with an IVF cycle, which involved injections to stimulate egg pro-
duction, extraction of the eggs, and fertilization in the lab. Fortunately, three of the fertilized eggs developed into viable embryos
and were transferred back to my womb, at which point I was sent
home to rest.

I moved deliberately and carefully, hoping not to dislodge any
embryos, hoping that at least one fertilized egg was attaching and
clinging to life. I prayed, I hoped, and I believed. On day two or
three, I had the distinct feeling of being settled, as if something
in me had come to rest.

Nine days later I went to the center for the blood test that
would determine whether I was pregnant. Greg and I agreed that
the wait for the call that day seemed endless. I willed the phone
to ring, and at the same time dreaded it ringing. When at last the

call came, I waited for the third ring before I picked up the receiver. My hand was shaking as I held the phone to my ear.

"Lauren, your levels have more than tripled," the nurse said. "They are heading in the right direction. Congratulations—you're pregnant!"

She cautioned me that I would need to take another test at week's end to confirm that the numbers were still climbing, but the most important results were in. We were finally setting sail on the voyage we had hoped above all to be making.

I called Greg. "We did it," I told him. "You're going to be a dad!"

Now that we knew the baby carriage would be filled, it was time to finalize our wedding plans. I felt that the most romantic thing to do, since we already had what mattered most—a baby on the way—would be to elope.

"Why not do what we want?" I said. "A wedding is about us, and we should make it our own. Let's do what feels right." We looked at each other and smiled. It would be simple after all: City Hall was just a few blocks north.

We decided that the most democratic way to inform our friends and family would be through the newspaper, so we submitted our wedding announcement to the *New York Times*. Someone from the *Times* informed us that the paper wanted to feature our nuptials in its weekly Vows section, which required that we name the person who would officiate, rather than simply report that we would be married by a justice of the peace. When we asked for a name from City Hall, the city clerk himself agreed to perform the ceremony in his chambers.

Our wedding day, March 8, 2000, was unseasonably mild. I

decided to wear a deep red and black wool bouclé suit by Christian Dior. The jacket was double-breasted with black buttons and featured a matching A-line skirt, which I wore with sheer black stockings and black patent Ferragamo pumps. Greg wore a solid black suit with a white shirt and a horizontal gold, blue, and black Hermès tie. Our two best men—Brian Clark, a cofounder of Euro Brokers, and Steven Moore, who ran I-Trade-Currency— were chosen for their friendship and proximity.

At lunchtime a shiny black Lincoln pulled up to the entrance to Tower One at the World Trade Center, and Greg ushered me into the waiting car. We headed north on West Street, made a right onto Vesey, and drove east to the gloriously ornate building at 1 Centre Street. It was Manhattan's first skyscraper, and I marveled once more at the lobby's vaulted, white-tiled ceiling, which was modeled after the Palazzo Farnese in Rome. When we arrived at the city clerk's chambers, we were ushered into a carpeted space with wood-paneled walls and dark red accents. A minute or two later, the *New York Times* reporter called to say that she'd been held up and probably wouldn't make it in time. Eager to get under way, we proceeded with the ceremony, pronounced our vows, and were married.

We glided out of the building. I held flowers in my arm and practically danced over to City Hall Park. The chief of the watch, the top cop on duty in New York City, walked by as we crossed Centre Street; smiling, he tipped his hat and said, "Congratulations." Our best men brought a bottle of Dom Pérignon and a pair of gold-rimmed champagne flutes, and we toasted our marriage in front of the fountains.

Afterward, we walked back to the World Trade Center and finished the workday. (It never occurred to us not to.) Our wedding had required just over an hour, and Greg's colleagues were quite amused when they learned he'd just been married. Not wanting to create a distraction, I told my coworkers nothing about it.

The next morning we left for Round Hill Resort in Jamaica, where we enjoyed a honeymoon in a beautiful villa tucked into the bluffs above Montego Bay. When friends and family learned of our surprise nuptials in their Sunday paper, they called to offer their congratulations. But as it turned out, not everyone was surprised: though we hadn't told them, our parents were wise to our elopement because the journalist who was writing the story for the Vows section had telephoned them the week before. The reporter must have been startled to discover that she had blown the surprise.

But now we had a much more important surprise to share with our parents. We let them know of their impending elevation to grandparent status by sending them small Gund Teddy Bears. A note attached to each bear explained that their future grandchild looked forward to getting to know them, and asked if they would please bring their little bear along when the time for their first meeting finally came.

I loved being pregnant. I had waited so long and wanted it so much, and now I felt unbelievably lucky. My pregnancy was easy and so uneventful that by the second week of October—a week after my originally scheduled delivery date—I still wasn't showing any signs of going into labor. After consulting with our doctor, we agreed that he would induce labor on October 26. I woke up that morning feeling great and worked a full day at the office. I remember looking out from the 105th floor toward the Colgate Clock across the Hudson in Jersey City at about 5:00 p.m. The clock had kept me company throughout my years at Cantor

Fitzgerald, and now I said to it, *Next time I see you, it will all be different.*

I went home at 5:30, and then Greg and I took a taxi to the NYU's Tisch Hospital, as excited as if we were going on a long-awaited vacation. My birthing room had a large TV on the wall, and when we arrived the Yankees and the Mets were playing the fifth game of the 2000 World Series. Greg was an avid Yankees fan, and I was one by marriage.

After I received my first medications, we relaxed and settled in to watch the game. Going into the ninth inning, the score was tied, but with a two-out single in the bottom of the inning, the Yankees won the game and were once again champions. For Greg and me, it was the perfect prelude to an even bigger celebration.

By the end of the game, I had begun to go into labor, albeit very slowly. About six hours later, at 6:25 a.m. on October 27, 2000, Tyler Jacob Manning was born.

"He's beautiful," I said to Greg as I cradled our son in my arms. "Can you believe we made him?"

Greg kissed me and kissed Tyler, and then I said, "Greg, I have never felt such love, such joy as I do right now."

My parents would be staying with us for two weeks, and they arrived at the hospital that morning at 8:30, thrilled to meet their first grandchild. They laughed like children, taking turns holding their grandson, just hours old. Tyler and I went home two days later, and even though we were still in the midst of an extensive renovation that would properly combine the two apartments, I didn't care. It didn't matter that the kitchen was in the bedroom, or that the dining room was a table sitting in front of the fireplace at the foot of our bed—we could have lived anywhere. What mattered was that we had a perfect, twenty-one-and-a-half-inch, seven-pound-two-ounce baby. While my mom cooked delicious meals and I rested, Tyler slept in his bassinet a scant five feet away.

The next few months were a blissful time, and the gorgeous summer of 2001 would echo in my memory for years afterward. Though we owned the weekend house north of the city in Pine Plains, Greg and I longed to be at the beach with Tyler, so in August we headed east to the Hamptons and shared a house with our friend Debra Walton. Greg and I took long walks on the beach in the early morning sun, with Tyler in the baby carrier and Caleigh, our Wheaten Terrier, barking at seagulls and chasing a tennis ball down to the breaking waves. We explored local haunts and lounged around the pool listening to Madeleine Peyroux's "Walkin' After Midnight," the Grateful Dead, and the Bob Marley *Legend* album. We'd crank the stereo under the bright August sunshine, and I would hold Tyler closely in my arms while I danced and sang along to Bob Marley's "Three Little Birds."

Don't worry, about a thing,
'Cause every little thing, gonna be all right.

Over Labor Day weekend we threw an end-of-summer party for a number of our friends. We played our summer standards with some Rolling Stones and 10,000 Maniacs mixed in, and we ate huge amounts of grilled vegetables, steaks, and seafood. On that perfect summer night, kids played, dogs romped, and we all laughed and danced under a bright white moon.

The happy glow of that memorable Labor Day weekend faded the moment we returned to Perry Street.

I knew Greg had been thinking about making a career change for years, and now he told me that he was seriously considering returning to journalism. I was stunned; how could he consider such a thing just when we had a new baby? I thought we were finally settled, finally building our family and our future. What I didn't know was that for several weeks he had been speaking to the managing editor of our industry's leading trade magazine about a possible position. Greg reminded me that the publisher of the magazine was hosting their inaugural Financial Technology Congress in a few days, and that he planned to attend the keynote breakfast, where the editor would be speaking. It was scheduled for 8:30 a.m. on September 11 at Windows on the World.

Greg was in so many ways the perfect complement to me. His interests, his habits, and his very essence had filled some void in me that had always existed. I scolded myself: How could I be so selfish? How could I doubt him? Some years ago, he had been a reporter for and then the managing editor of Telerate Energy Service, and before that he'd been the executive editor for the University of Pennsylvania's college newspaper. If he made a concerted attempt to get back into journalism, he would almost certainly make a successful transition.

Even so, my practical side asserted itself. *Hold on*, I thought. *Reporting is a job for a young person willing to live on a shoestring, travel anywhere, and do whatever it takes to gain traction. Journalism is a profession best suited to someone who has no one to think about but himself, and now we have Tyler.* With a preacher's zeal I began to implore Greg. "Please don't do this," I said. "I don't want to start all over. I don't want to be responsible for making most of our income." A reporter's job would pay only enough to cover our apartment's maintenance fees.

Our argument began at the very end of that Labor Day weekend, and it picked up speed as the conference at Windows on the World approached. Every night after we put Tyler to bed, we would settle into the living room and soon find our conversation returning to the same painful topic.

"You have a family," I would say to Greg. "You can't make the same decisions you might have ten years ago. You have responsibilities."

"I told you the first night we dated that someday I intended to make a change."

"But you had years to make the switch, and you didn't."

"I never found the right opportunity before. Now I might have a chance to use what I've done for the past ten years to make the transition into something I might do better."

I imagined Greg working for one of the drab industrial newsletters that almost no one read. What kind of an opportunity was that?

I shook my head in frustration. "But Greg, you can't abandon your family to make a start in a profession that doesn't pay well."

"I won't be abandoning my family, just making a change I've talked about for years."

"A change that would mean you'd make less money."

"Yes, there's no question I'd have to take a pay cut."

Eventually we'd retreat to our respective corners to brood. I was sick over it. One part of me wondered what I could be thinking. I had everything: I loved Greg, and I had a beautiful baby, a home, and a career. I had a wonderful life! Why did I doubt my husband's dreams? But another part of me feared that we would lose it all if Greg made a bad career decision. My vision of the future—a vision I thought we shared—required both of us to contribute equally. Suddenly I felt like a spectator watching my own life. I could see how fortunate this woman was, but somehow her life seemed empty.

On Monday, September 10, I came home from work at six o'clock. Tyler greeted me at the door, all smiles in red jean overalls with a short-sleeve white shirt underneath. Our nanny, Joyce, raised him up, and he lifted his arms for me to take him. I held him, kissing his cheeks while we laughed and whirled around the room. He was all giggles. After a final swirl I put him down and told Joyce I'd be back in a moment. I went down the hall and slipped on a pair of jeans and a lightweight short-sleeved sweater. I bid Joyce good night, turned on the stereo, and started dinner while Tyler played on his mat. Over and over, he built two towers of wooden blocks and then delighted in knocking them down. As quickly as he could build the towers, he would knock them down.

I gazed out the window, the blue sky trimmed with emerging orange as the sun began its descent. The Hudson River was ablaze with rippling light, and the silhouettes of the low-slung buildings of Hoboken were dark against the horizon. Our apartment faced west, and as the sun set over the river the light came almost horizontally into our apartment. Every clear day of the year the sunsets were beautiful, one of the main reasons we loved living on Perry Street.

That night I was preparing a quick dinner of broiled salmon and French string beans. I was still trying to adjust to motherhood, maintain my career, and provide a touch of Martha Stewart on the side. Knowing that Greg would be home soon, I thought about our ongoing argument and found myself chopping the ends of the beans with extra force, as if wielding the knife would somehow help quell my rising anger. I was sure we would soon be continuing our discussion about his career, and I had no doubt that it would come to a head before the conference the following morning.

Greg walked in the door at about seven, and we coolly said hello to each other. I still hoped that he had had an epiphany and realized how crazy his idea was. After I poured two glasses of a white burgundy, I served the food and we sat down to eat. The dinner table provided neutral territory: Tyler sat in his highchair between us, and Caleigh was, as usual, stationed underneath his chair, waiting for the inevitable rain of crumbs and tasty tidbits.

It was a beautiful night, so after dinner we put Tyler in the stroller, attached Caleigh's leash, and headed out for a walk. Caleigh wagged her tail and body as if she hadn't been out in years and practically pulled us out the door. We crossed West Street and began to walk south down the path of the emerging Hudson River Park, flanked by newly planted grass and berms filled with an assortment of pines, crepe myrtles, and flowers. The river was to our right, its dark water shimmering and undulating like a blanket covered with shining jewels, and as the sun fell toward the horizon, the sky was filled with rosy pinks and oranges. A mile away, the brightly lit, ever present towers of the World Trade Center rose above the city, dominating the skyline.

The tranquil setting belied the winds of resentment rising between us. Like a slowly gathering storm, our argument picked up the dirt and debris that inhabited the dark places in our hearts and began to build.

"If I don't do this now," Greg said, "when will I ever do it? You know I'm running on fumes. I feel like I drag myself to the office every day."

"But you have an obligation to your family. You'd be forcing me to support all of us on my own."

"I won't be shirking my obligations, Lauren. You've known all along that I want to do this. Now that I have a chance and I'm looking at it seriously, you're acting as if you've never heard the concept before."

"So what if you talked about this idea years ago!" I shouted. "You don't have that luxury now, Greg. You have to earn a living! Write on the side, but keep your day job."

He looked down at me and said, "It's not going to work that way."

"Oh yes, it will!" I said. "I can't believe that you would tell your wife you're going to quit your job right after she's had a baby."

"You want me to hate my job for the rest of my life?"

"No, just find a different one that isn't a step backward."

"Another job in the data business?"

"If that's what it takes."

"That's so you, Lauren. You want the life you want, period. It's like you never listened to me."

I couldn't believe he was talking this way, with Tyler riding in the stroller directly in front of us. Our lives were only just beginning, and now, suddenly, the dual burdens of my father's role as provider and my mother's as homemaker were about to come crashing down on my shoulders.

"I listened to you," I said. "But your actions spoke louder than your words."

"I never said I changed my mind."

"But we decided to have a family. We decided, Greg. You can't abandon your family this way!"

"I am not abandoning my family!" he shouted back. "I'm looking to do something I can keep doing for the rest of my life."

"But can't you see that if you do this now, you'll be abandoning your responsibilities as a father?" Furious, I turned to him. "You never wanted a family! That's it, isn't it, Greg?"

"You know I wanted a family, Lauren."

"You're not the man I thought you were when I married you."

"I'm exactly the man you thought I was."

"I can't believe I'm married to you."

"I can't believe I'm married to you."

With that, the argument ground to a halt, and we walked on in near silence, anger seething as dusk settled more deeply and we turned for home to put Tyler to bed.

The battle continued later that night—back and forth, back and forth, with no resolution. Sitting in the far corner of our bedroom, Caleigh cowered and shook.

Finally, worn out, we stopped, emptied of words. With a sick feeling in the pit of my stomach, I went to bed and fell into a deadened, dreamless sleep.

3

DECIDING TO LIVE

You don't get to choose how you're going to die, or when. You
can only decide how you're going to live now.

—JOAN BAEZ

The flames were consuming me, and as the first searing pain hit,
I thought, *This can't be happening to me.*

The fire embraced my body tighter than any suitor, touching
every inch of my flesh, clawing through my clothes to spread its
hands over me, grabbing left and right, rifling over my shoulder
blades, down my back, wrapping my legs in agony, gripping my
left arm, and taking hold of both my hands. I covered my face, but
I could not scream. My voice was powerless. I was in a vacuum,
the air depleted of oxygen, and everything was muffled. The
screams, the roar of the fire, the shattering sound of breaking
glass—all that was very far away. I was suspended in space.

Then my captor slammed me forward. I lurched toward the
doors in a desperate effort to get away. As I did, something—I
have no idea what—hit me in the back of the head. For a moment,
I was pushed against the glass; then I was sucked backward again
by a monstrous inhalation that pulled me toward its heart. I battled

to escape, fighting my way through the outer doors as the fire grew over me, spreading farther down my head, my arms, my back, my legs. Then, abruptly, I was spit from the fire's mouth out onto the sidewalk, where I had been standing just seconds before.

The fire was all around me now, a shroud of flame. I was suffocating with every gasp of charring fumes. I saw nothing but concrete and pavement, but I knew there was a narrow strip of grass on the other side of West Street, in front of the World Financial Center. I knew with absolute certainty that I had to get there, that the patch of grass offered my only chance to put out the flames, and that if I did not push myself toward it with a razor-edged act of will, I would be annihilated, devoured by unbearable pain and terror.

I felt myself sliding toward blackness—and then something primal rose up from the deepest part of my being. My mind was flooded with a vision of Tyler.

I can't leave my son. I haven't had him long enough. I can't abandon him. I can't go out like this, running across the street in flames to die in a gutter.

All my strength was now focused on a single goal. I had to reach that strip of grass.

Without breaking stride I was already running toward it. I could think of nothing else. As I came off the curb, one of my ankles turned under me and snapped. I felt a momentary crushing sensation; for a split second, the focus of my pain shifted, and then the fire took over again. I pushed myself over the cement median. The journey seemed to last for hours.

Oh my God, I can't believe this is happening. This pain can't be real.

I prayed for death, in that unspeakable way that people who are experiencing unimaginable pain can. As if summoned, Death seemed to be running beside me, dancing and beckoning, smelling of burned cloth and flesh. But I didn't believe that even Death would deal a final blow to the pain and end my agony.

I reached the grass and dropped down. I began to roll. A man came charging across the grass toward me. He ripped off his jacket and used it to help smother the flames, and as he bent over me, he became the focus of all my pain and anger.

Shouting, I implored him to get me to a hospital, to please help me find a way out of this hell. I told him Greg's cell phone number and yelled at him to call Greg. "Tell him to get down here and help me!"

At least three or four others had also reached the grass. At first they'd been screaming, but now they were silent and lay motionless on the bank. I saw more people start to pour out of the tower, some stunned, mouths agape in shock, others screaming in horror.

My clothes had been incinerated or torn away. I was writhing in pain, but my adversary's prolonged and intimate assault was only just beginning. The burn enveloped me, squeezing tighter and tighter. Though its flames were extinguished, its boiling venom was spreading, moving deeper and deeper, its pincers tearing through layer after layer of dermis, fat, and muscle. I twisted and turned, trying to escape, but it kept me effortlessly in its grasp, a weightless force with infinite strength to hold on to me. The pain intensified, breaking upon me in pounding waves, each threatening to send me under.

The air was filled with noise, but I was in such agony that I heard only vague, distant sounds: the impact of objects slamming into the ground, the sirens of emergency vehicles, the grinding thunder of bending steel and breaking glass. Far above, a dark cloud belched from the punctured sides of Tower One with such velocity that the tower seemed to cut through the blue ocean of sky, trailing a deep, black scar in its wake. It seemed so incongruous that the same force that tore a gash so high up on the building could have created the fire that engulfed me in the lobby so far below.

The pain kept burning through every ounce of my being. I prayed to somehow climb out of my body to escape it. I rocked back and forth in a futile effort to break free. Again I felt myself losing hold, as if my fingers were being pried off a ledge one at a time as I dangled over an abyss.

I pleaded with God: *I can't leave, I can't leave my son. I haven't had enough time with him. I worked so hard to have him. I can't leave him now.*

The impulse to let go grew overwhelming, and I knew I had to push beyond the seductive veil of softness that offered to envelop me and usher me deeply into the bowels of death. My eyes closed, and once again I saw my son's face.

Had it all been in vain? The thought that my love for my son might not be enough, that I might fail to return to him and to all those who needed me, was devastating. I knew I had to do everything possible to get back to him. This was it, the moment when I had to fight to hold on with the last full measure of my strength.

I decided to live.

I was not conscious of its approach, but the roar of the second plane drew my eye, and I looked up just as its tail section vanished into the South Tower. The immense pain skewed my perception; improbably, I found myself wondering how part of a plane could be hanging out of the building. But after it hit, I knew that this was not just an accident. They had come back for us.

The man who had covered me with his jacket stayed with me

as more agonizing seconds ticked by. Never abandoning me, he remained by my side, talking to me, anchoring me. I didn't realize it, but I had already been lying on that patch of grass for twenty minutes. The cloud of gray-black smoke rose ever farther into the sky. The sheer walls of the World Trade Center seemed to veer and sway, their parallel lines of steel and glass confusing my depth perception, triggering vertigo and a sense that the building was moving toward us. More objects thudded to the ground. I had a terrifying sense that the building was leaning and about to topple over on us.

"Get me out of here, get me out of here!" I yelled, pleading with my companion. "We have to move over! It looks like the building is going to fall!"

He helped me rise, and we moved a few feet down the bank. I told him I wanted to look down at myself; he implored me not to. But as we reached the new spot I sank forward onto the ground, and I clearly saw part of my body for the first time. At the ends of my arms, my wrists and hands were resting upon the bright green blades of newly planted grass. They were perfectly formed, perfectly shaped, and every detail was sharp. Yet something was terribly wrong. Against the verdant background my hands were pure white, as if dipped in wax or sculpted from white marble.

"Is my face going to be all right?" I asked my companion.

"Your face is okay," he answered.

I had continually asked him to call Greg, and he had dialed Greg's cell phone repeatedly but received no answer. Finally I realized that Greg must still be at home. Miraculously, he had decided not to attend the breakfast and keynote speech at Windows on the World after all. Early that morning our next-door neighbor, who had just had major foot surgery, asked if Greg could help her leave her apartment so she could run an errand, and he had agreed to assist her before heading to work. Now I gave my companion our home telephone number and shouted at him again, "Call my husband. Get him down here to help me!"

Time seemed to have stopped. Seconds had become eternal. The pain continued to rip through my body, rolling in on giant waves, rekindling itself in a steadily fiercer, ever-escalating, seemingly boundless extension.

"Where is the ambulance? Where is the ambulance?" I yelled.

The sirens of emergency vehicles were incessant but always far away, blending into a dissonant cacophony. A few ambulances had driven by us, though none had stopped. The next time a siren seemed to be coming in our direction, my companion jumped up and began to run toward it, but the sound quickly faded.

Yelling through the pain, I implored him to get me to the Weill Cornell Burn Center. Somehow, I knew this was where I needed to go. He seemed ready to try to take me; he had his keys out of his pocket and was turning as if to go get his own car when, at last, on the northbound side of West Street, an ambulance pulled up and stopped, its lights flashing. This was my last chance out. I was certain that I would die on the side of the road if I didn't make it onto that vehicle.

I must return to my son.

The EMTs jumped out, but then headed toward the building, away from us. Understanding that they would not be coming for me, I began to rise up off the grass. My companion helped me get to my feet and supported me as we started slowly back across the street, now littered with debris, toward the ambulance. With his help, I somehow managed to get there, but even now I have no idea how I walked that impossible distance.

———————

Once aboard the ambulance, I was placed on a stretcher on the floor. Others who were less seriously wounded climbed aboard around me and crowded onto the benches that ran the length of the cab on either side of me. Within a couple of minutes the ambulance was overflowing. I felt as if I'd landed in a military transport that was loading battlefield casualties. Above me was a din of moaning, screaming, crying. Some people had broken limbs, others deep wounds. Profligate amounts of blood were everywhere. I lay in the canyon between them, flat on the collapsed gurney, surrounded by their torn trousers, soot-covered shoes, and bare, bloodied legs. From their front-row seats they observed my medieval torture with pure and absolute fear in their eyes. I could see it in their faces, and I felt it in my gut.

Lying there in a vortex of pain, a misbegotten, forsaken mess wedged into a small space on the floor, I began pleading, "Please, please help me." It hurt so much—I desperately wanted them to make the pain go away. But the EMTs didn't respond. Instead, they frantically stepped around me to help the others. I was not being given fluids or any sort of attention. I could see that I'd been pegged as a goner. The act of boarding the ambulance would be my finale.

Beneath the burning pain I began to feel a cold, blue rage. The living would move on; clearly they didn't see me as one of them.

In a fury, I yelled, "Get this truck the hell out of here!"

Nobody answered. I saw that bits of clothing were still smoldering on my body. The people sitting on the benches kept stealing glances downward, obviously uncomfortable with the closeness of my suffering.

But one pair of eyes did not look away. A woman—later I would learn that her name was Mrs. Rivera—was seated next to her husband. Both of them were peppered with glass fragments from the revolving door that shattered around them when the fire blasted into the lobby. She yelled to the EMTs, "Please, some-one help her!"

One EMT came over, and I heard him tell Mrs. Rivera that they didn't have a burn blanket. A few moments later, someone placed a jacket over me. And then, fifty minutes after the fireball exploded out of the elevators and engulfed me, the ambulance at last began to move me away from the burning towers.

I became aware of being somewhere where there were walls, and then I came to understand that I was in a hospital. The ER doctors gathered around me wanted to cut off my rings and my watch. I pleaded with them not to, and somehow they managed to slide my wedding band and my engagement ring off my fingers.

I had been brought to Saint Vincent's Hospital at Seventh Avenue and Eleventh Street in Greenwich Village. Greg had been to its emergency room several times; now it was my turn.

Lying on a gurney, I was taken up to the tenth floor, where I was given fluids and a handheld intravenous pump through which I could self-administer morphine up to the maximum safe dosage. But by this point my hands were covered in bandages, and they were so badly burned that I couldn't move my fingers to press the button. Unbelievably, the pain was getting worse, spreading as if someone were pouring boiling water on me over and over, or strip-ping every bit of my skin off my body. It simply didn't stop. There was no reprieve, no way to evade the waves of agony that racked my body.

Nearly mad with pain and anger, I was passing in and out of awareness. But still I remained conscious, and I could hear every-thing being said by those around me. I realized that the nurses were on the phone with Weill Cornell asking about burn protocol.

"What the hell are you doing?" I shouted at them. "If you don't know how to treat me, get me out of here and up to Cornell! You don't know what you're doing!"

As the doctors and nurses looked down at the abomination in front of them, their confusion and panic were obvious. It was not their fault, but they really didn't know what to do. My burns covered more than three quarters of my body. I was in need of specialized care, but instead I had been admitted to a general critical-care floor, where I was sharing a room with two other patients. Neither my doctors nor my nurses had experience treating serious burn injuries.

I looked up at the ceiling. Everything seemed to be growing dimmer. I felt myself shrinking farther into nothingness, into oblivion. I was becoming a nonentity in the eyes of the living. Though I wanted to stay with it, the world was leaving me behind.

Ever since learning that Tower One had been hit by a plane, Greg had been pacing from room to room in our Perry Street apartment, pounding the wall with desperate uncertainty, calling out my name. He dialed me repeatedly, but my office line was always busy and my cell phone never rang through. He went back and forth between watching the television coverage of the attack and going out on our terrace, from which he could see the World Trade Center and the vast black hole in the side of North Tower. He tried to convince himself that I was still alive.

He felt a strangling helplessness. Where should he go? What should he do? Several times he left the apartment and got as far as the sidewalk, only to turn around and return upstairs. Finally he made the calculated decision to wait. If he ran downtown and entered the maelstrom at the Trade Center, the chances of finding me were infinitesimal. He had left his cell phone at the office the night before, and he realized that if anyone was trying to find him, the only place they could reach him would be at home.

At 9:35 a.m., the phone rang once and then went silent. A moment later it rang again. Greg snatched it up, and a man's voice on the other end said breathlessly, "Mr. Manning, I was with your wife. She's been badly burned, but she's going to be okay. We got her on an ambulance."

"Where are you taking her?" Greg demanded. But the call cut off, and no one answered when he tried to call the number back.

At 8:30 that morning, my mother and father had been sitting at the breakfast table in their home in Savannah, Georgia, working on a new crossword puzzle. As the sun streamed over the lagoon behind their house and lit their breakfast room with its soft southern light, CNN droned in the background. At about 8:50, my parents became aware that CNN had interrupted its broadcast to show a plume of black smoke pouring from the World Trade Center. A moment later, they learned that a plane had hit several of the higher floors in the North Tower. They knew that was precisely where I worked.

My parents listened in disbelief, and then my father turned to my mother.

"I think we lost her, Joan."

My mother began to dial my work phone number and then Greg's, encountering busy signals at both our offices. She also tried and failed to reach us on our cell phones. Finally she called our home telephone. She was hugely relieved when Greg picked up the phone, but then Greg told her that although I was alive, I had been seriously injured.

"I got a phone call saying that she was badly burned, but that she's on an ambulance," Greg told her. "I don't know what hospital she's being taken to." He also told her that he didn't know what condition I was in.

It was not yet 10:00 a.m., but every flight in the United States was grounded. My parents immediately grabbed a few belongings, got in their car, and started driving toward New York.

After what seemed like hours but was actually just twenty-five minutes, Greg received a second phone call about me. This time a woman's voice calmly said, "Mr. Manning, this is Saint Vincent's Hospital. We have your wife here."

After thanking her, Greg hung up the phone, sprinted out of the apartment, and ran the eight blocks to the hospital.

When I saw Greg enter my room, my anger spoke first: "Call Mitch and get me to a fucking burn unit!"

Greg came to my bedside. Looking up at him, I told him what had happened: "Greg, I was on fire. I ran out. I prayed to die. Then I decided to live, for Tyler and for you."

The pain jolted me again, the waves now seeming to come every second, beyond what I could imagine or bear. I was close to tears but wouldn't let myself cry.

Swathed in sheets, my head wrapped in bandages, I asked Greg the same question I had asked my companion on the grass an hour earlier.

"Will I be okay?"

"You'll be fine," he said.

He spoke with confidence, his tone even. His reassurance gave me some peace for the first time that morning.

"How does my face look?"

"It just looks like you're really tan."

He didn't tell me that massive blisters were forming on my upper lips and chin, or that my hairline was a black-burned crisp at the top of my forehead. He had no idea what the rest of my body looked like, but it was obvious to him that I had been burned very badly. Gazing down at me, he was shocked, but he didn't show it.

I asked him what had happened. He confirmed that a plane had hit Tower One. I asked him if everyone at Cantor Fitzgerald was okay. He avoided giving me an answer, but of course he knew.

"My hands are no good," I said. I told him about the morphine drip. "I can't press the button." Then my rage started to speak again: "Get me to a burn unit; these people don't know what the hell they are doing! Why can't they see that I can't use my hands!"

Greg immediately told the nurses to give me the morphine, explaining that it was impossible for me to administer it to myself. Then he hurried to the nurse's station and called our friend Mitchell Blutt, a doctor, on his cell phone. He reached Mitch at the airport, where his flight had just been canceled. Mitch was deeply concerned and offered to provide any assistance he could, but at the moment there was nothing he could do to help.

Greg began pressing the attending physicians, asking whether the nurses were doing the right things and providing the right level of care. The doctors, who had been regularly consulting among themselves, attempted to be reassuring, but despite their efforts it was obvious to Greg that they were figuring things out as they went along. Greg pleaded with them to transfer me to Weill Cornell, but they told him they couldn't, that the entire city was in lockdown.

Greg returned to my room, deeply concerned but still projecting confidence. At one point an orderly wheeling a cart of linens entered and then stopped in the middle of the room.

"What's that smell?" she asked, crinkling her nose.

"That's her skin," Greg replied.

Clearly no one on the staff was familiar with serious burns, but a few minutes later Greg successfully insisted that I be given a room all to myself.

The social worker on the floor had watched this drama unfold, and around lunchtime she went down to the hospital chapel to pray for me. When she emerged from the chapel she saw a group of people gathered in the hall, medical personnel who had come off the street to volunteer. She walked over to them.

"I need burn nurses."

Two women stepped forward. The social worker was certain that they appeared in answer to her prayer.

Minutes later the two nurses entered my room on the tenth floor. One of them told Greg, "She is going to be given a sedative so that we can start giving her burn care." They said they would remove all the bandages, clean and treat the injured sites with silver sulfadiazine cream, and then rebandage me until the next round of care. Greg asked how long it would take, and they told him that it would last one to two hours. Then, gently, they told Greg that he needed to leave the room.

Greg came back to my bedside, leaned down, and spoke to me again, his tone gently reassuring. He told me that these two nurses knew what they were doing and that they would take good care of me.

At this point, though, I was frantic with anxiety over the fate of my colleagues at Cantor Fitzgerald. Before Greg walked out of the room, I asked sharply, "Did you call Gary?"

Confused, Greg asked if I meant our contractor. But I was referring to one of my colleagues.

"No!" I shouted with annoyance. "Gary Lambert!"

Those were the last words we shared for almost two months.

It was 2:00 p.m. I had been living with monstrous pain since 8:46 that morning, but now, more than five hours later, I was finally sedated and sent beyond the burn's crushing grip.

The two nurses went to work. Greg stayed with me a moment longer and then left my room as instructed. As he did, he turned and took a last look at me. The nurses had raised me up and begun to remove my bandages. He saw most of the skin on my back hanging down in grilled, blackened flaps.

Greg walked down the hall to a sparse elevator lobby, which had a single pay phone on the wall. He dropped into a chair. The hospital had been closed to all but patients, their immediate families, and medical personnel. Outside the building, growing crowds had begun a solemn vigil, but inside, he was mostly alone.

After sitting in stunned silence for a few moments, Greg stepped to the pay phone and used our telephone credit card number to call Joyce, who told him that Tyler was fine. Then he called Wendi, our next-door neighbor, and learned that both towers had collapsed. After hanging up, Greg walked down the hall to a south-facing window and saw a cloud of smoke far downtown. His eyes searched the sky, but he wasn't sure where to look. The landmark buildings were gone; our offices were nothing but empty space.

Greg took the elevator to the hospital's first floor to find some food. Walking through the halls, he passed scores of people standing in the waiting areas, all of them spellbound by the news playing on the televisions. Most of those watching appeared to be hospital employees. For a few minutes he stopped and watched the live coverage along with them; then, weak with shock and exhaustion, he sat down against a hallway wall.

Later, after he returned to the tenth-floor elevator lobby, Greg tried to decide which of his colleagues to call. He feared that no matter whom he called, he would hear the anguished wails of families mourning their murdered loved ones. Yet with his first call he reached Brian Clark, one of the two best men at our wedding. Miraculously, Brian had survived and made it home, even though he'd been working on the eighty-fourth floor of the South Tower when it was hit. Brian told Greg the names of several colleagues at Euro Brokers who had survived, and then began to recite the names of others who were already known to have died.

At about 3:45 p.m., the nurses told Greg that he could return to my room. Standing at my bedside, he was relieved to see that due to the sedation I was no longer suffering from the pain. As the afternoon wore on, he continued to query the doctors and push them to have me transferred to a burn unit. He also asked for more information about the severity of my injury; the doctors told him that by their estimate I had suffered burns over 60 percent of my body, although many seemed to be second-degree. Greg knew that second-degree burns could heal on their own, and so, despite the terrible burns he'd seen on my back, he allowed himself to hope that the situation wasn't as bad as it looked. But the doctors' estimate, he would soon learn, was completely wrong.

At 5:00 p.m., Greg was somewhat surprised to see a doctor he recognized walking toward him down the hallway. A year earlier,

I had taken Greg rollerblading for the first time; the outing was a complete success until he tried to sit down on a bench to remove his skates, at which point he fell and suffered a compound fracture to the middle finger of his right hand. At the Saint Vincent's Emergency Room, he'd received a splint and a referral to Dr. Edmund Kwan, whom he had visited for a consultation. Greg remembered Dr. Kwan as calm and thoughtful, and now he was once again a reassuring presence as he told Greg that he had written an order to have me transferred to New York-Presbyterian Hospital Weill Cornell Medical Center, where he had secured a bed at the William Randolph Hearst Burn Center.

Greg had consistently been told that a transfer was impossible, and in the past hour or so he'd come to believe that my chances of surviving were steadily dwindling. Dr. Kwan's order for the transfer was the best possible news; at last I would be getting the care I needed.

Soon afterward, a pair of EMTs from West Nyack, New York, arrived and began to prepare me for transport. Dr. Kwan had also written an order to increase my sedation so that I could be intubated.

"We have to give her ventilator support so she doesn't have respiratory failure and die in the transport," Dr. Kwan explained to Greg. "We need to support her breathing."

One of the EMTs produced a bag-valve ventilation device, and he explained to Greg that he would manually squeeze the bag at regular intervals until I was delivered to the medical staff at the Burn Center.

"I am going to breathe for her," he told Greg.

The preparations took almost an hour, but finally I was ready to be moved. I was placed on a gurney, and the EMTs brought me down to the lobby and then outside. As my gurney was wheeled slowly across the sidewalk to the waiting ambulance, Greg saw hundreds of people lining the streets surrounding the hospital, staring in silent vigil from behind wooden police barricades. Twenty or more empty stretchers sat in neat lines on the sidewalk, waiting for patients who would never come.

Greg sat in the passenger seat beside the ambulance driver for the trip to Weill Cornell. As the truck headed across Fourteenth Street and drove north through Manhattan, it was waved ahead by uniformed personnel at each intersection. The streets were empty of traffic, and Greg experienced a ghostly feeling as the ambulance moved through the silent city. Finally they reached the ER bay at New York-Presbyterian, where the surreal quiet remained. The only sound as I was wheeled to the emergency entrance was the creaking wheels of the gurney.

We rode the elevator to the eighth floor and then turned right. As we entered 8 West, the Weill Cornell Burn Center's critical-care wing, Greg noticed a tall man dressed in green scrubs. Hair askew, eyes wild, the man glanced at our little procession, turned to look down the hall, and screamed, "Next!" I was wheeled into a glass room, where eight doctors and nurses surrounded my bed to assess and then begin to treat my burns. Once again, Greg was asked to step out.

It was now about 6:00. In the brightly lit hallway outside the room, Greg watched a uniformed firefighter cheerfully set down a huge red cooler filled to overflowing with ice and bottled water. The cooler made a strange impression: it was as if the entire day had been an outsized corporate picnic.

Invited by the nurses to help himself, Greg grabbed one of the bottles of water and walked down the hall. After passing through 8 West's automatic doors, he sagged into a chair in another nearly empty waiting room.

A few minutes later, a chaplain came out of 8 West, approached Greg, and asked, "Are you all right?"

"Not really," Greg replied.

"It's your wife?" the chaplain asked.

"Yes. She was badly burned at the World Trade Center."

The chaplain sat with Greg. A few minutes later, our longtime friends Mary White and Bill Fisher arrived and joined him.

Sometime in the next two hours, a doctor came out to the waiting room and informed Greg that they would need to circumferentially graft my left arm in cadaver skin or I risked losing it. Greg proceeded to sign the first of many surgical consents.

Bill and his wife, Marian, lived just a block from the hospital, and around 10:00 p.m. Bill persuaded Greg to come to their apartment and try to get some sleep. With some hesitation Greg accepted, but almost as soon he reached their apartment, Greg told Bill and Marian that he had to return to the hospital. Bill came back with him, and together they pulled some bedsheets from 8 West's linen closet. Sleeping little, the two of them spent the night on the harsh tile floor of the waiting room.

By that time, the increase in sedation had put me in an altered state and sent me on a different kind of journey. I entered an arid dreamscape of rocky cliffs and faceless people, where, beneath blackened skies, amid a cold and brooding darkness, I would engage my adversary in a relentless battle for my life.

4

DARK WORLD

Out of the night that covers me,
Black as the Pit from pole to pole,
I thank whatever gods may be
For my unconquerable soul.
—WILLIAM ERNEST HENLEY, FROM "INVICTUS"

When I was growing up, my grandparents lived nearby in Hawthorne, New Jersey, at the top of a steep hill. Across the street the hillside fell away, opening up to overgrown wild grass bordered by woods crowded with thickets of thornbushes. The neighborhood kids loved to explore there, and Billy, my grandmother's neighbor's son, was no exception.

Billy was the kid we all remember from our childhoods—the one who just couldn't shake trouble. As many times as we should have known better, we believed the stories he told us. So when he said that money was buried at the bottom of a steep slope of wood and underbrush, we were eager to go find it.

One afternoon, my sister, Gigi, and I decided to explore beyond the perimeter of our typical escapades. We took large walking sticks with us, and as we ventured into the thick brush, Gigi started out in front of me. Not content to follow, I pushed ahead and got in front of her; as the older sister, I wanted to be first in line for discovery, and I considered it my duty to serve as the front line of protection. This jockeying for position continued throughout our childhood and would become one of its most enduring legacies.

Soon we entered a thicket of wild rosebushes that formed a natural trellis above our heads, and we had to hunch down in order to pass through. The dense, thorny foliage seemed to grab at our clothing, but since this path might lead us to Billy's buried loot, I was determined to be the first to see it. Suddenly I felt a sharp stinging on my arm, and within seconds my entire body became raw with pain as I was pounded by scores of darts. I had walked straight into a massive wasp's nest, over a foot in circumference, that was attached to the underside of one of the bushes. Flailing wildly at the cloud of wasps that swarmed around me, I turned and ran, ignoring the thorns that tore at my skin as I tried to escape the stinging insects. Gigi, once again in front, fled up the hill ahead of me, yowling as she scrambled through the underbrush. Remarkably, she had not been stung, not even once.

After running up to the road and then across the street to my grandmother's house, we flew into the kitchen, where my grandmother and mother were sitting at the table having a cup of tea. My grandfather and father, hearing the racket, bounded up from the basement. By then, my body was covered with red welts—I had been stung well over fifty times. My mother was alarmed but quick to comfort me. My grandmother found some calamine lotion and mixed a baking soda paste that she and my mother slathered over my stings. Her eyes wide, my sister watched my arms and legs begin to swell, our little treasure hunt all but forgotten. Fortunately, that was the worst of it.

One year later, the blessing of my need to be first became strikingly apparent when, at a Memorial Day party at our house, a bee lodged under my sister's bracelet and stung her on the wrist. Within moments, as Gigi came crying to my mother, she began blowing up like a pink Pillsbury Doughboy. The swelling immediately traveled to her hand, and her wrist was soon so swollen that the bracelet she was wearing became immovable. She started wheezing, and her breathing became erratic; within minutes, her pulse slowed and she was in danger of asphyxiating. My parents rushed her to the hospital, where doctors were able to stabilize her. No one had known it, but Gigi was highly allergic to bee stings.

For years afterward, this became a running joke: I had done Gigi a big favor by being the bossy older sister and shouldering her aside just before we'd encountered the wasp's nest. Had she been first when we went down the hill and into the rosebushes, she would not have been around to laugh at the joke. In our family lore, I had earned a badge of merit for taking the hit for her that day.

Now I had suffered a much more serious attack, but this time it was no accident of nature, and no amount of calamine lotion was going to help me. In fact, my doctors were deeply concerned that I might be beyond help of any kind, and during the first six weeks of my hospitalization the likelihood of my death loomed large.

Soon after I arrived at Cornell's burn unit on September 11, I was put into an induced coma from which I wouldn't fully awake for weeks. That night I underwent the first of dozens of operations; doctors opened the burned skin along the length of my left arm to relieve swelling. The first seventy-two hours, known as the *resuscitation phase*, were critical; burns covered over 82 percent of my body, most terribly on my back and left arm. Burn specialists estimate the recovery rate for victims of a fire to be 100 minus the percent of the burn, which meant that I had about an 18 percent chance of surviving.

As Greg kept a vigil beside my bed, I lay quiet, wrapped in white bandages, the only sounds the hiss of the oxygen supply and the rhythmic function of the ventilator feeding the breathing tube I held between my front teeth. My face and body were bloated because I was being pumped full of vital fluids in a critical attempt to replace the vast amounts of fluid I was losing through my burns. Even when looking straight at me, Greg found me unrecognizable

Greg was especially worried about my hands, and in the very early days he would ask the nurses to let him listen to the Doppler sonar readings from my wrists, the tinny heartbeat sound with a frothy background noise that parents associate with a fetal heartbeat. In this case, the sonar confirmed that blood was flowing to my hands. That steady ping was one of the biggest early breaks I caught on my long road back; it was another sign that my body was working hard to heal itself, postponing the day when doctors would have to perform surgery on my hands. Every day of natural healing gained was a blessing.

When Greg left for the evening, the nurses caring for me looked at him with a compassionate but serious expression; only later did he realize that they believed I had almost no hope of surviving. But they, too, understood their job: they would do everything possible to prevent me from dying on their watch. Their vigilance would be absolute and total.

On Thursday, September 13, Greg met for the first time with Dr. Roger Yurt, the medical director of the Burn Center. Dr. Yurt would supervise my care, and he calmly described what I faced. The following night, Greg had a second conversation with Dr.

Yurt, and this time he was joined by our friend Mitchell Blutt, the doctor who had been stuck at the airport when Greg called him on the morning of 9/11. Speaking in layman's terms, Dr. Yurt began by providing a "knee bone connected to the thigh bone" explanation of my care.

Mitch, who had previously been an attending physician at New York-Presbyterian, asked, "Medically, what's her condition?"

Dr. Yurt provided one in just a few seconds.

Mitch turned to Greg. "You shouldn't be happy, but you should be pleased. Lauren has survived the resuscitation phase—that's a great piece of news."

Greg now understood that I had lost significant ground during the hours at Saint Vincent's, but the transfer to the Burn Center had made it possible for me to survive the critical first three days. Even so, my odds would not improve significantly for many weeks. As Dr. Yurt had explained, severe infection and other complications would present a deadly threat; not until my burn injury was "closed" would I be out of danger. In another daunting calculation, the days to closure typically equaled the percentage of the burn, which meant that if I survived I would almost certainly remain in critical condition for nearly three months.

From that point forward, Greg always requested that he be given the medical description of my treatment; he worked hard to understand the more technical aspects of my case and so have a better grasp of the challenges I faced. But there was one conversation he was very careful to avoid. He had heard about the formula that doctors used to calculate a burn victim's chances of survival, but he made it clear to everyone that he did not want to know either the formula or my odds. He preferred to view my situation in the simplest terms: if I was still breathing, I still had a chance.

But the next evening, just before midnight, Greg was about to leave the hospital when he met Dr. Palmer Bessey, the Burn Center's associate director, in the hallway.

Exhausted and nearly sick with worry, Greg couldn't help himself. "What are her chances, according to the formula?" he asked.

Dr. Bessey paused a moment. "Do you really want to know?"

Greg realized he didn't. "No, I don't."

"Well, I can tell you her chances are less than fifty-fifty," Dr. Bessey said.

Greg nodded, but instinctively he sensed that my odds were far worse.

"She's hanging in there pretty well," Dr. Bessey continued. "She's going to get sicker before she gets better, but we're going to do everything we can to pull her through. I don't want those bastards to get another person."

The next afternoon, sitting at my bedside, Greg recalled the conversation with Dr. Bessey. Looking at my closed eyes, my swollen face, and the breathing tube emerging from my clenched teeth, he had the sense that I was already shrouded and at peace, already an infinite distance away from him. Overwhelmed, he confronted the possibility that the last few days of my life might be spent sedated and wrapped in white webbing and that my last memories would be of the pain and horror of being consumed by fire.

It was a vision of such emptiness that when he returned to the waiting room, he began to shake and cry uncontrollably. His first instinct was to leave the room, and he took a short walk to recover himself. But when he came back feeling no less inconsolable, he was approached by Karen Waizer, whose husband, Harry, was an attorney and one of two other Cantor Fitzgerald patients on the unit. Karen was maintaining her own anxious vigil about the fate of her spouse, and she suggested that Greg speak with Rabbi Andrew Jacobs, who had come to the hospital from their synagogue in Westchester to visit with her.

Rabbi Jacobs, an unassuming young man wearing a *kipa*, a dark suit, white shirt, and tie, sat with Greg and took his hand. Greg told him he was losing hope that I would survive and so felt helpless with despair. But since the doctors had told him that I could hear spoken words, Greg asked the rabbi to come to my room and pray by my bedside. Greg told him that although I would not understand the words, I might somehow recognize that the rabbi was speaking in a holy language.

Greg and Rabbi Jacobs walked down to my room, and as they stood by my bed, the rabbi told Greg the Hebrew word for a person fated to be bound to another from birth: *bashert*. Greg then spoke the word to me, and as he did he began to feel calmer. Later, when Greg left my room, he believed that despite his imperfections and limitations as a man of God, he had somehow done something for me. Having looked for God and found an answer, Greg never again faced a moment of doubt like that one.

For the first nine days of my recovery, Greg stayed at a friend's apartment nearby and was never more than five minutes from my bedside. Manhattan remained in lockdown; there was no way to get from place to place except by public transportation. If Greg had gone home and I'd taken a turn for the worse, he might not have been able to return to the hospital before I died.

Joyce, our nanny, didn't leave Tyler's side for the first twenty-four hours. For the next two days, she went home late and came back early, and Tyler slept at the apartment of two close friends of ours, David and Kelly Halpert, who lived a block away from us and had two young boys of their own. David and Kelly also had two dogs, and they generously offered to take care of our dog, Caleigh, for as long as necessary.

My parents, meanwhile, had driven from Georgia to New Jersey in one very long day. That first night, they stayed with Gigi at her home in New Jersey; the next day, they took public transportation into Manhattan and moved into our apartment on Perry Street, where they would stay for the next three months.

Before my parents made their first visit to the Burn Center, Greg asked a doctor to have a short conversation with them in a conference room; he felt they should be briefed on the gravity of my condition and prepared for what they would see. He also asked the doctor to explain to them that I would be able to hear their voices, and to encourage them to speak to me in the most positive and optimistic tone they could muster—anything to buoy the part of me that still maintained an awareness.

That first trip to my bedside was very difficult for my parents, but they were both very brave and maintained their composure. After the visit, my father left the room, walked down the hall, and allowed himself an agonized sigh. My mother, though she remained reserved and self-possessed, fell into a chair and seemed to disappear into herself. From that moment on, my parents somehow managed to steel themselves and respond to this terrible crisis with the same immense resilience that they had shown throughout my life.

Greg took the night shift and assigned my parents the day shift, ensuring that someone from my family would be with me for at least twelve hours a day. In the weeks ahead, Greg and my parents would be a constant presence, and I believe that I did hear their voices and know that they were there for me.

In the days and weeks following my injury, I was receiving triple or quadruple the normal doses of narcotics to control my pain. Over a short period of time, these drugs create a tolerance that requires increasingly larger doses to achieve the same effect, and at points the nurses could see that despite the narcotics my agitation was almost ready to burst through to awareness. I was switched from one drug to another in cycles to maintain the necessary level of pain management. On a regular basis, I would be taken off morphine and put on fentanyl, then switched back to morphine, then back to fentanyl.

Throughout, my mind was extremely active, and I have vivid memories of what I can only describe as a dream state. But to call that long sojourn beyond consciousness a dream or even a nightmare cannot possibly capture the breadth and power of what I experienced.

Skirting the hourglass, broken in time, nothing remains.

I pass into a world of jagged mountains, an arid land broken by mighty cliffs that are bathed in half-lit grays and tans. The cliffs plunge into caverns filled with stalactites and stalagmites. Beneath the caverns is a bottomless abyss.

I wander alone, seeking the paths to safety. It is a cold and desperate netherworld, the sky always dark, treacherous. Ashes, dust, blackened rock—traveling through a barren, lifeless place, I am on an odyssey to an unknown destination.

I live in dry, rock-filled crevices deep in the mountains, icy caves where hard, biting edges sear my skin. I am the prisoner of an unseen army, and a malevolent presence stalks me, seeking to destroy what strength I have.

In mortal danger, I am desperate to escape. Leaving a darkened catacomb, I crawl forward, dragging myself toward a cliff. An invisible force shoves me over the edge. I flail at the gravel in an attempt to cling to the rock, but inevitably I fall, plummeting downward, my belly weak, my mind reeling with the sickening sensation of a free fall with no parachute.

I tumble through the air certain that I will never stop falling, flying, twisting through the dark gray sky. I try to grab the edges of cliffs, the breath gone from my lungs, fear ripping out my insides.

Miraculously, at the last possible moment, I land on another ledge. Worlds of people are living on these cliffs, all of them wearing exotic tunics and faded robes. Amid the forbidding atmosphere of a lawless street market, I wander through clanging alleyways full of carts and unintelligible chatter. But here too the dark presence is chasing me, and I crawl through a series of bazaars in terrifying slow-motion flight, just beyond the reach of its grasping claws. The rocky ground is gray and dry; dust whirls upward as I scramble across it, my legs seemingly weighted down by chains. At last I am cornered at the cliff's edge where, inevitably, I am cast off again.

A week after the attacks, my condition had stabilized to the point that my doctors were able to take a crucial step on the perilous road to recovery. On September 18, I underwent the second of dozens of skin graft surgeries, though it was the first operation using skin harvested from my own body.

The main risk to me—as is the case with anyone who is severely burned—was infection. Skin provides a barrier to countless bacteria, and when the skin is damaged, the body's immune defenses are drastically weakened. For this reason burn centers maintain positive pressure in a patient's room; whenever the room is open to the hallway, the flow of air is always outward, never in. Because my skin was so badly damaged, the majority of my body had no natural protection. Grafting skin onto the burned areas would therefore be a race against time, which is why Dr. Bessey had told Greg during my first days in the Burn Center, "She's going to get sicker before she gets better."

Cadaver skin had been used as a temporary graft for my left arm, but no permanent graft is possible without the use of a patient's own skin, called an *autograft*. This is why it is so difficult to survive extensive burns: the same graft sites have to be harvested a number of times, and each site has to heal before it can be used again. In my case, doctors had few areas of healthy skin to work with; for this first autograft, they removed skin from the front of my body and then used it to graft the backs of my legs and most of my back. Eventually, the graft sites would include all the undamaged areas of my body, including my scalp. Fortunately, the layer of skin that is harvested is so thin that I was able to retain all my hair.

I was also very lucky to be athletic and relatively young. Even more important, my lungs and stomach were functioning well, which meant that my oxygen intake and my protein intake, both of which were critical to my body's self-repair, were still supporting me. As my body surged into a hypermetabolic state trying to repair itself, my body temperature and my heart rate rose. (For months, my resting heart rate would be more than 130 beats per minute, nearly double the normal range of 60 to 80 beats per minute.) The amount of fuel needed for this effort was huge: the feeding tube delivered six thousand calories a day to my stomach, far more than I would have been capable of consuming.

As Greg himself later wrote, burn care is a broad engagement against a range of injuries, all of which have to be managed. The body is used as a blunt instrument to fight the causes of death, and all its systems are taxed to the utmost in a desperate effort to keep the patient alive long enough to have a chance to recover.

When Greg wasn't at my side, he spent long hours in the waiting room. As anxious as he was about me, he was also grieving for the scores of people he'd known who had been killed. His company, Euro Brokers, had lost sixty-one employees, most of whom died after the second plane slammed into their trading floor. It was a miracle that Greg himself hadn't died: only the last-minute phone call from our neighbor had kept him from attending the breakfast and keynote speech at Windows on the World.

Of all the businesses and organizations with offices in the World Trade Center, my company, Cantor Fitzgerald, had suffered the most grievous losses. We had occupied five floors in Tower One—the 101st floor through the 105th—and since all of them were above the point of the first plane's impact, everyone on those floors had been trapped. Thousands of people working for other firms had escaped before the towers fell, but no one working in Cantor Fitzgerald's offices had made it out.

Though Howard survived—he had been taking his oldest son to his first day of school—his younger brother Gary had perished. Edie Lutnick, Howard's older sister, received two phone calls from Gary that morning. When he called the first time, she hoped that it was to tell her he was safe; instead, he was calling to tell her that he, too, was trapped in Cantor's offices. The second time, Gary was calling to say good-bye.

Approximately one thousand Cantor employees had worked at the World Trade Center; in the days after the attacks, those who remained scrambled to determine how many employees had been in the building at the time of the attack and how many had safely evacuated. The firm issued a statement in which Howard spoke of the "very difficult and confused situation" and promised to do everything possible to find out what had happened to each of the company's employees.

In time, we would learn that 658 employees had died. Edie would become the executive director of the Cantor Fitzgerald Relief Fund; wearing a different sweater of Gary's every day to keep his memory close to her, she would oversee the effort to help support both the families of Cantor's victims and the families of dozens of other workers and visitors who were there with them that day.

Cantor Fitzgerald would survive this terrible blow, but for now my company was nearly in ruins.

As the days went by, the Burn Center became a focus of the city's outpouring of grief. People were desperate to do something, anything, to salve the wounds suffered by the attack's survivors and to provide support to their loved ones. Strangers visited the waiting room bearing care packages and hoping to offer solace. Colleagues from Cantor Fitzgerald and Euro Brokers came to sit with Greg; both Howard and Gil Scharf, the CEO of Euro Brokers, paid visits to the Burn Center during the first few days. When a young woman who had worked for me and given me a copy of *The Runaway Bunny* as a baby gift came by, Greg gave her a teddy bear that the counseling staff had insisted he take for himself.

Volunteers brought food and magazines to families in the waiting room. Cards and banners from elementary schools, prayerful messages from churches, and get-well notes addressed to the families and to the hospital workers began to flood in from people around the country. Thousands of handmade cards were hung on the hospital walls and eventually given permanent frames.

Also pasted on the walls—and on thousands of buildings and lampposts in the city—were countless posters featuring photographs of the missing, put there by families desperate to know the whereabouts of their loved ones and hungry for any information about their last moments.

As time went on, the crowd in the waiting room grew smaller. One by one, several of the most severely injured patients died; the next day, the chairs their families had occupied for weeks would suddenly be empty. Soon only a handful of 9/11 patients remained in the burn unit. Still fighting for our survival, we were among the very small group of catastrophically injured victims who had escaped or been evacuated before the towers fell.

The families of the other patients in the Burn Center came to the hospital day after day, and Greg bonded with them as they shared news and helped each other through ups and downs. But death stalked the waiting room, creating an undercurrent of dread when they discussed who was stable, who was doing better, and who had taken a turn for the worse. Greg sat with one woman on the night her friend died; he also spent many weeks with the family of Jennieann Maffeo, who died on October 22, and whose family offered loving prayers for me after her funeral. Greg attended the funeral, and Jennieann's sister Andrea told him, "Lauren is going to make it. Jennieann will be the last one to die—you won't have to go through this."

On September 23, I was taken for my first visit to the tank room, where I was placed on a foam-covered, stainless steel slab illuminated by six bright lights. Using six hoses positioned above the slab, four or five nurses scrubbed me with caustic soap and gauze to clean and debride my wounds, which involved removing damaged tissue so that the healthy tissue that remained would have the best chance to heal. Because of the size of my injury, this meant scrubbing large areas that were nothing but raw nerve endings and exposed blood vessels that were trying to regenerate new tissue. I would continue to endure these treatments for my remaining two and a half months at the Burn Center, but even while in an induced coma, the experience of being treated in the tank room left a profound imprint upon my consciousness.

The risk of infection was always extremely high, so whenever anyone entered my room, they were required to wash their hands and then don sterile gowns, sterile gloves, and surgical masks. This included visitors as well as Burn Center staff. Visits were restricted to immediate family members, with a single exception. One day, Howard insisted on being allowed to visit me, and Greg agreed to bring him into my room for a few minutes. Howard washed his hands, put on his gown, gloves, and mask, and stood beside me to tell me that he and everyone at Cantor Fitzgerald loved me and were praying for me to pull through.

Meanwhile, I had more graft surgeries on my feet, my hands, my fingers, and my backside. Doctors cross-pinned knuckles in both my hands so that my hands wouldn't lose the small amount of functionality that remained. Every few days I seemed to experience yet another life-threatening crisis. At one point, I developed a profound infection from Acinetobacter, a hospital-borne bacteria that lives in the hospital itself, stalking the weak and debilitated. My face and my body swelled pink with sepsis. When I did not respond to the first round of antibiotics, the doctors had no choice but to treat me with the most powerful antibiotic available, one that brought a serious risk of kidney failure.

On September 30, Dr. Yurt sat down with Greg and told him what needed to be done.

"Is this a crisis for Lauren?" Greg asked.

"Yes," Dr. Yurt replied, using the most serious tone he would use during my entire stay at the Burn Center. "It is."

But I survived that crisis, and as September turned to October, I continued to "hang in there." In an effort to keep family and friends posted about my progress, Greg had begun sending out frequent updates by e-mail, and soon his beautifully written notes were being disseminated across the country and around the world. The response was stunning. A family friend contacted her priest in Ireland and asked that a prayer be said on my behalf; that priest in turn telephoned a number of other priests in Ireland and asked the same. Before long, congregants in churches all over Ireland were asking God to protect and keep me. Bushels of get-well cards and rosaries began to accumulate in my hospital room; I even received blessed water from the Kabbalah Centre and holy water from Lourdes.

Word of my fight to live began to attract media attention as well. On October 17, the *New York Times* published a front-page article about me called "A Fireball, a Prayer to Die, Then a Hard Battle to Live." Among those who commented for the story was Howard, who said: "She's got to pull through, because she's got 700 families' worth of love. It's not fair, but she's part of their hope." The article prompted a huge response from readers, as well as another wave of gifts, cards, and messages of support. Much later, Greg would tell me about the *New York Times* piece and say that he cooperated with it in large part because he wanted Tyler to have a record of my fight for life, a conversation that moved me to tears.

A month after my injury, I remained heavily sedated, my body constantly pushed to the edge of its capacities. Numerous chest X-rays—I would ultimately have a total of forty-seven—showed fluid in my lungs and in my chest cavity, and despite the ventilator I had regular episodes of erratic or inadequate breathing. On October 9, after four full weeks of biting down on the breathing tube, I underwent a tracheostomy, which allowed doctors to move the tube from my mouth to the base of my neck.

The most dangerous phase of my recovery was ending, and although I continued to battle infections, my healing had progressed to the point that I could be brought, gradually, closer to consciousness. My eyes would open intermittently, and images began to blend with the sounds of the voices I had been hearing. Reality began invading my dreams.

My breath, misty and heathered, courses through plastic tendrils that threaten to choke me as much as breathe for me. I feel air being pushed into my lungs, but they don't want to work. Breathing is such a heavy burden. "Breathe slowly," someone says, "breathe deeply. Lauren, you must breathe more deeply and slow down your heart rate."

Images of monitors form a procession, accompanied by an unending chorus of beeps. I want them to stop. But whenever I slow down my breathing, the incessant beeping only accelerates.

I tumble into a vivid dream about my mother's parents. In this dream, I am somehow living with them, even though I'm not yet born. It's the holidays, around 1940. An ornament falls off the Christmas tree and breaks, landing on a small box containing a toy. Fire erupts, I feel the flames on my skin, and suddenly they are everywhere. Though I am badly injured in the fire, no one knows. Then it is years later, and on winter walks to the park I wear fine clothes, gloves, a black hat, and cashmere coat with a fur collar to hide my disfigurement. I am living at the top of a hill, and my grandparents' house is down below. Every day I venture out in hopes of seeing my grandparents again. Only once do I see my grandfather; he stands in front of me holding the toy box in his hands.

Now I am being taken to a room that contains a four-foot-deep, eight-foot-round vat filled with warm water. Someone guides me into the water and gently bathes me. The bath feels comforting, sooth-ing, healing. I return often to this bath chamber, but one day I take a single glance at my arms and see how burned they are. I breathe in haltingly, my stomach weak with what I have just seen.

I begin to feel certain dread when I return to this place, because now the chamber brings only pain. To bring me here, someone opens up the floor beneath my bed; once it's parted, I am mechani-cally lowered into the chamber by a series of pulleys. The lights in the room are blindingly bright, and once in the bath, I am washed off with a hose that tears at my skin.

It is so hard to breathe. Someone keeps asking me to breathe slower, more deeply. I keep trying, but I can't. I have a breathing tube in my throat, and I have such a hard time breathing that I just want to stop. I plead with my doctor to pull the tube from my throat and put it in my stomach—I am sure I can breathe through my stomach. But he refuses.

My doctor flies to the hospital each day, landing in a helicopter on the roof above my head. He visits me often, but one day he leaves me after I again plead with him to remove the tube. Moments later, the wind is whipping through my room, and I hear my doctor's voice above the roar of the helicopter as it awaits his departure. He is on the roof with the other doctors, counseling them. "Do it," he says. "She may as well be comfortable since she's probably not going to last." I feel sad when I hear that, but I'm also pleased that some-one has finally agreed to do what I've asked.

I call out for my mother. Somehow I'm sure she has seen me on

TV; I try to get a message to her, begging her to come save me. But it doesn't work; nothing is working. The bandages I have had on for so long are finally coming off, but still no one will help me. Someone is always nearby, yet no one ever comes to rescue me.

While my body fought to remain among the living, it veered on an almost daily basis toward death. The metronome of my breathing would falter, my body would begin to shut down, and those caring for me would once again launch a frantic effort to save me. My guardians—my husband, my parents, and my doctors and nurses—helped to prevent death from stealing me, but only by the narrowest margin. For weeks, their prayers and potions built a barricade that kept death at bay.

Meanwhile, alone in my netherworld, I sensed that the last phase of my solitary struggle was beginning. I felt the demons clawing their way into me, burrowing, infesting my being, deceiving me from within, and seeking to coax me toward a final capitulation. They almost had their way, and the infections, the collapse of my lungs, and the worrisome blood tests were all testimony to the epic battle whose decisive round was raging within me.

But at last I was growing stronger, and I would not bow.

There is no defense in life except the courage of your heart to prevail, and I decided: *I will outlast my adversary. I will find my way home again to the house by the river, and my pain will be swept away by the tides of the sea.*

5

AWAKENING

You gain strength, courage, and confidence by every experience in which you really stop to look fear in the face. You must
do the thing which you think you cannot do.

—ELEANOR ROOSEVELT

Toward the end of October, I was gradually brought out of sedation over a period of days. Haltingly, I reemerged into the conscious world. I had no clear memory of how badly I'd been hurt.
I felt something in my throat and knew I couldn't speak, but I
didn't know why. I had no idea how long I'd been asleep.

One day I opened my eyes, turned my head, and saw Greg's
face. He gently smiled and said, "I love you." Light streamed in
through the window behind him. I glanced around. To my left, a
thicket of plastic tubes ran from a metal trolley down to various
parts of my body. I breathed in and felt an obstruction in my
nose. Each time I inhaled, a chilly draft pushed into my throat.
Shifting my head a bit, I realized that something was sticking out
of my neck. It was the ventilator tube, which entered my windpipe through a tracheostomy hole in the base of my neck. Nurses

poured into the room, joined by a doctor or two. I didn't understand. Why were so many people coming to see me? What was
going on?

Greg said, "Lauren, you've been sedated for a long time. You
were badly hurt, but you're going to be okay."

Of course I would be okay—why wouldn't I be? Besides, hadn't
Greg just told me this at Saint Vincent's? I realized I was in a
hospital, but I assumed I'd have to endure only a short stay. I
didn't know what day it was, but somehow I felt confident that I'd
be allowed to go home by week's end. Strangely, though, neither
Greg nor my doctors would tell me when I'd be leaving. Then again,
they really weren't saying much at all, which struck me as odd.

Gradually I began to realize that something wasn't adding up.
For one thing, I was almost completely immobilized. For another,
the simple act of breathing required tremendous effort. Why was
every breath such a challenge?

At some point two physical therapists came in with bandages,
plaster, and a big pot of water, and then set them down on the
floor. They combined the plaster with the water to form a paste,
dipped the bandages, and carefully molded plaster casts to my
legs and feet. These casts, the therapists told me, would serve as
splints and keep my legs in functional positions.

My new "boots" bore more than a passing resemblance to
those that might be worn by the Bride of Frankenstein and were
just as graceful. They weighed six or seven pounds apiece, and
since I hadn't used my muscles in so long, it was impossible for me
to move my legs. But my plastered legs weren't meant to be moved;
the purpose of the splints was to preserve my ranges of movement
until I was well enough to move my legs on my own.

For the same reason, the therapists also encased my arms and
hands in plaster. Now I realized why it was so difficult to move: I

was bandaged from head to toe. Perhaps I wouldn't be going home
at the end of the week after all.

As the heavy sedation wore off and I came to full consciousness,
I struggled to accept the fact that this unending torture and pain
was my new reality. My psyche ached as much as my body. Though
surrounded by people who were trying to help and support me, I
felt terrifyingly alone. The liquid food that was being pumped
into me through the tube in my nose invariably made me extremely
nauseous. What I wanted more than anything was ice, but I
couldn't have it and had no voice to ask for it anyway.

Since I had suffered internal damage to my windpipe and had
the ventilator tube in my neck, I couldn't speak. Since my badly
damaged hands were bandaged and strapped into splints, I couldn't
push the buzzer and summon a nurse. The only way I could com-
municate was by banging my arm casts against the metal bed rails,
so when I needed help I would just knock a cast against the rail—
click, click, click—and look to my nurse for assistance.

Tubes and wires sprouted from just about every orifice and
every part of my body. I was connected to the world through plastic and wires, and a plethora of monitors recorded my moment-
to-moment progress. Watching the lines moving across the small
screens surrounding me, I felt as if I were gazing at a lightshow
during a psychedelic rock concert. Up and down, left to right they
scrolled, fading at one edge only to appear again at the opposite
edge a moment later. The monitors recorded my heart rate, blood
pressure, and blood oxygen, and other machines delivered oxygen, food, and water to my body.

Especially painful was an IV line that regularly needed to be
removed and reinserted on the inside of my upper inner thigh.

This was one of the few areas of my body that remained unscathed by burns or skin grafts. But the veins there had already been so overused that some had collapsed, and those that remained had to be pushed and prodded before a new needle could be reinserted. Keeping that line in good working order was vital to provide medications or administer anesthesia when I was sent back to the operating table.

As the days passed, I began to comprehend the severity of my injuries. Both of my hands remained wrapped in bandages that were inches thick. My left hand was three times larger than my right hand. When the bandages slipped, I saw a graft of cadaver skin on my left hand that resembled a slab of raw meat. Metal pins that had been placed in the joints to stabilize them protruded like silver nails shot from a nail gun. The fingertips, peeking out beneath the ends of the bandages, were pencil-thin and black. I could not imagine how what I was looking at would ever be a hand again.

From the moment I opened my eyes, my mother and father became my partners in recovery. They came to work promptly every morning, arriving at the hospital ready to engage in whatever activity was necessary to help me. Their presence meant the world to me, especially because the early phase of my recovery was so difficult and traumatic. Suddenly as helpless as a child, I was forced to relearn such basic skills as sitting up, standing, and taking my first steps. But this strange recapitulation of our long-ago roles made my parents' presence calming and familiar.

Just as they did when I was a child, my parents responded to each new challenge in a straightforward, matter-of-fact way. They were so well-grounded that as a girl I sometimes found their steadiness annoying. Whenever something awful happened, they always reassured us that we would be okay, that we'd all survive. Whether coping with the death of one of their parents or responding to a creosote fire that erupted in the chimney of our childhood home and threatened to engulf our house in flames, they never lost their composure or panicked. Not even when we returned to our house after some time away and found it in shambles because burglars had ransacked it and lived in it for days. My parents met every crisis with focus and determination, and they never worried about what they could have done differently or about things they couldn't control. They simply went to work on solving the problem in front of them.

Like many members of their generation, my parents had never been particularly demonstrative. When I was young, I couldn't understand how they never seemed to be caught up and swept away by a swarm of unruly emotions. It amazed me, for instance, that when my brother began choking at the dinner table one night and had to be rushed to the hospital, they acted instantly but were as methodical as if they were EMTs themselves. At times I had felt suffocated by their reserve, but now I recognized it as a quiet inner strength that was helping them keep their balance despite what had happened to me.

Yet something in their behavior was subtly different. During those arduous days in the hospital, I began to see a side of them I didn't know existed. My mother was uncharacteristically supportive and upbeat; instead of the stern demands for proper deportment I had so often heard, she consistently offered me an easy smile that showed great tenderness. My father's behavior surprised me even more. One morning I woke up and saw him standing at the end of my bed, tenderly massaging my feet, looking distressed. He held them in his large hands, sending ripples of deep warmth through me. "I just wanted to get the blood moving," he said. "They felt so cold." Then he looked up at me, the uncertainty of my fate lodged in his eyes, and said, "I love you, sweetie." I couldn't remember him ever saying those three words to me. I turned my head away, overwhelmed by his show of emotion. Closing my eyes because I didn't want him to see my own fears, I said, "Thanks, Dad. I'm going to be fine."

I was so moved by my parents' kindness and expressions of love; their commitment to seeing me through this terrible time helped me enormously. And hearing those simple words from my father also provided unexpected closure. They healed a wound I hadn't known existed, one that must have been open for many years. Though I had always known that my parents loved me, now I finally felt truly beloved, and this gratified me in a way I had never experienced.

Various kinds of therapy were essential to my recovery, but the sessions in the tank room were the worst. That vision from my nightmare world had been very real: during my first visit to the tank since regaining consciousness, I once again encountered the bright lights and the metal slabs and the water that hurt. The process of debriding my wounds was extremely painful, and there was no avoiding it. I would look down at my arms where the skin grafts were still healing and think, *Oh my God, I can't believe this happened to me.*

I was taken to the tank room every day, and at first I wondered why I couldn't visit that big, gentle pool of warm water I recalled from my dreams. But I soon learned that this comforting pool had indeed been a dream, because in reality the water was never gentle. Every time I went to the tank room, the pain was so extraordinary that medication was needed to dull its intensity. Without it, debridement would have felt like being operated on without anesthesia. During one session I was given ketamine, a powerful drug that caused me to hallucinate, which was a horrific experience.

After the debridement in the tank, I would be brought back to my room and lifted onto my bed again. Exhausted, I would lie there feeling violated by the breathing tube, the feeding tube, and all the other tubes and lines running into my body. But soon it would be time for the next round of therapy, which involved getting a new set of plaster casts.

Without this therapy, I risked permanent loss of important ranges of motion. When the body remains immobile for long periods of time, it tends to atrophy, and since my hypermetabolic state put me at special risk for muscle wasting, that tendency was amplified by orders of magnitude. And if my muscles atrophied too much, they would be unable to counter the constant pulling of my tendons. The splints' job was to hold my feet in their functional position as I lay sedated; otherwise, they would pull into a pointed down, pigeon-toed rest position that might make it impossible for me to ever take a normal step again.

This physical therapy was so important that even while I was sedated, the Burn Center's therapists had visited once a day to exercise my limbs for me through limited ranges of movement, including sitting me up, reaching with my arms, and raising my legs off the bed. After one of those sessions, a therapist told Greg that I had several times resisted her movements with surprising strength. Since the movements were quite painful, it wasn't surprising that even though sedated, I had resisted them by reflex, but the therapist was encouraged because my response suggested a physical strength that she felt would be a huge asset during my rehabilitation.

Now I was awake to feel the pain from the splints and the physical therapy sessions, as well as the pain from my surgeries. All the skin on my back was now grafted, and during the initial surgery the fatty tissue beneath it had been excised as well. Meanwhile, thick layers of bandages covered my buttocks, the site of the most recent graft. Fortunately, most of my surgeries had gone well, though the most difficult sites—such as the buttocks and elbows, which were involved in nearly every motion—took the longest to heal.

It was difficult to see much humor in my situation, but occasionally Greg and I would find something to laugh about. One day, for instance, Dr. Yurt observed that the surgery on my back was a good example of liposuction done the hard way. (Okay, you had to be there, but it *was* funny.) And as the occasional jokes suggested, we were gradually becoming accustomed to this awful situation. I was not out of the woods, but by now weeks had passed and what would have been unimaginable on September 10 became unsurprising. As time passed, Greg and I accepted my circumstances and tried to find occasional reasons to laugh.

Soon things that might once have been horrifying became merely annoying, and what would ordinarily be surreal became little more than odd. One day I heard a strange crackling noise; turning my head, I saw that my pillow seemed to be dirty. At first I was upset that the nurses and the aides had been so careless. How could they have given me such a dirty pillowcase? But then I realized that what I thought was dirt was in fact the flaking remains of my burned left ear. The pieces that had fallen off were crackling on the pillow when I rolled my head to that side.

I was also reduced to extremely primitive forms of communication. Since I couldn't yet speak, I was given a placard that permitted me to convey a few simple thoughts and feelings. On one side of the placard was a boxed alphabet that made it possible for me to spell out words. Next to that were the front and back outlines of an androgynous body, below which there was a red lightning symbol with the label PAIN. Supposedly this would allow me to easily identify where I was feeling pain, but it might have made more sense for me to indicate the part of my body that occasionally *stopped* hurting. On the other side of the placard were boxes with drawings and labels: DOCTOR, NURSE, HOT, COLD, WHAT TIME IS IT? and the ominous CAN'T BREATHE.

When I would mouth words, my mother would often understand what I was trying to say, but Greg almost never would. Pointing to letters in order to spell words was also difficult since the heavy bandages on both my hands and the heavy plaster resting splints made it impossible to be precise. One day Greg was stumped when I spelled what he thought was *ANKS*. He thought I was asking him to thank someone—a nurse or a doctor—and he kept asking, "Who?" Over and over I would shake my head, at which point he would guess wrong again. Finally, after I pointed to the television a few times, he realized that I was spelling *YANKS* and asking about the World Series game the night before.

Though we did share a light moment now and again, Greg and I both knew that I was still battling for my life and that the hard work had only just begun. And because the clock had never stopped ticking, the daily sessions of physical and occupational therapy never stopped either. I needed to work relentlessly at building up my mobility, because my tendons were constantly trying to tighten and with every passing day my scars were hardening a little more. The goal of my therapy was to increase my ranges of motion step by step, and the ultimate outcome would be limited only by my tolerance for pain.

Especially at risk were my hands, where the damage to the small muscles and joints had already required joint fusions and caused significant loss of tissue. Even when my fingers were still swollen from surgery, my therapists fashioned new splints that expanded my ranges by forcing my hands into more aggressive rest positions. During therapy sessions they aggressively manipulated my hands and fingers to the limits of what I could manage, and then carefully and incrementally they pushed beyond those limits. The pain was excruciating, but I knew that the rehabilitation of the complex anatomy of my hands had to go forward if I was ever going to regain meaningful functionality.

As Scarlett O'Hara famously said at the end of *Gone with the Wind*, "Tomorrow is another day." Sometimes, after yet another harrowing operation or a particularly bad session in the tank, that sentiment was about all I had to cling to. My life had collapsed into the immediacy of now. Breathing, moving, getting an IV line or a tube changed, grinding through the daily occupational and physical therapy—these, along with the twice-daily nursing shift change and the frequent measurements of vital signs and organ function, were the rhythms of my new life. I had no choice but to adapt.

It meant a great deal to me to receive cheering visits from Greg's family and from my own. Greg's sister, Pam, traveled from Lake Worth, Florida, with Greg's mother, Liz, and my niece, Emily. His stepsister, Laura, who lived in Fort Lee, New Jersey, was a regular visitor. My younger brother, Scot, traveled from Durham, North Carolina, and Gigi, who lived in western New Jersey, made frequent appearances, which never failed to raise my spirits.

When Gigi first visited me in the hospital after I woke up, she walked through the door clothed in the requisite surgical cap, sterile gown, and booties. I looked at her, my face brimming with a smile. She looked so vibrant and beautiful.

"I thought you could use some of these things," she said, beginning to unpack lotions and other personal items that she knew would make my hospital room seem a bit more like a home. There were very strict limits on what could be brought into sterile areas, so although my room was bright and sunny, it was sparsely furnished and decidedly institutional. Among the items Gigi brought me were a CD of Johann Pachelbel's Canon in D Major and two thick white binders.

Moving a chair close to my bed, Gigi sat down to show me the binders. Both binders were covered with a page carrying the title "Prayers and Loving Thoughts for You." Below the title was a picture of the sun shining through clouds, and the page was inscribed with a lovely passage from the work of the Roman poet Horace, titled "A Wish."

Health to enjoy the blessings sent from heaven;
A mind unclouded, strong;
A cheerful heart: A wise content;
An honored age; and song.

Gigi stood up to place the CD in the music player, and in a moment the room filled with Pachelbel's achingly beautiful music.

Then she sat back down beside me and opened the first of the binders. Inside were hundreds of notes and cards sent to me by my friends, by friends of our family, and by complete strangers from around the world. I had no idea that so many people knew about me and my battle to live. As Gigi read their thoughts and prayers, I experienced an almost physical sense of being lifted. My breathing became clearer and more deliberate. The gauzy haze that had been clouding my mind began to clear. As I scanned the gentle loops of handwriting from so many generous souls, I felt held and protected. My isolation in the burn unit had been so painful, but now I realized that I had been not been so alone after all.

Gigi removed one card from its clear plastic sleeve and handed it to me so I could read it more closely. This card was from her. Made of hand-pressed paper, with dried flowers scattered throughout, it was bound with a strand of yellow string and held a second card inside. When I opened the second card, I found the text of "The Story of Two Very Different Sisters," a poem by Laurel Atherton. Had the words been her own, Gigi wouldn't have written it any differently.

> One lives here, one lives there. One is a little taller than the other. Two different colors of hair, two different outlooks on life, two very different views from their windows. Both have different tomorrows ahead . . . Each has a separate destination and a distinctly different path to get there. But . . .
>
> For all the things that might be different and unique about them . . . these two sisters will always share so much. They will always be the best of family *and* friends, entwined together, through all the days of our lives. Their love will always be very special: gentle and joyful when it can be, strong and giving when it needs to be, reminding them, no matter how different their stories turn out . . .
>
> They share the incredibly precious gift of being "sisters."

This was indeed our story. The great distance between the paths we had followed could have separated us forever, yet as I traveled from the darkness of my world to the lightness of hers, we were somehow finding our way together again.

Tears welled up in my eyes, as they did in hers. She kissed my forehead, and I felt a current of joy course through my body. Rising from deep within me, it joined me with my sister. No longer was one of us in front, the other behind; now we were truly joined, two sisters side by side.

By early November I was fully alert but still unable to speak. I knew I was gravely injured, that my body and my life would never be the same, but I was possessed by an almost unbearable happiness. I understood how incredibly lucky I was to have survived and felt almost absurdly grateful to be alive. More than ever, I wanted to live, and, someday, to go back home and be with my family.

On November 14, Dr. Yurt announced that it was time to remove my breathing tube. I felt both anticipation and fear at the prospect of resuming breathing on my own. Dr. Yurt performed the simple procedure, and as the last of the tube came out, my exhalation was so powerful that the final plastic connector that had been lodged in my neck shot across the room. Dr. Yurt then placed a covering over the hole in my windpipe so it could begin to heal. By closing the tracheostomy hole, the cover also enabled me to begin to vibrate my vocal cords and so begin to speak for the first time in almost two months.

The removal of the breathing tube was a crucial milestone: it was the first measured step toward regaining control over my most basic functions. When Greg walked into my room that evening, I whispered, "Hi, Greg."

Startled, Greg stopped and looked at me. "Are you talking?"

"Yes," I said, nodding.

"God, that's wonderful."

That same night brought the other consequence of having my breathing tube removed.

While I was on the ventilator, regular suction was necessary because the breathing tube diverted the flow of air, and fluid that would normally evaporate instead built up in my mouth and throat. The need for suction would persist until the tracheostomy was fully healed, and not until then would I finally be able to breathe normally. For weeks, the gurgling fluid in my throat made me feel that I was continually choking.

Since awakening, I had not been sleeping well, in part because of that fluid. Every night I would think to myself, *Just one more hour.* I would pray to God, *Please, get me through the next moment.* But that night, shortly after my nurse left the room, Greg stepped out for a few minutes before going home. Suddenly I felt as if I couldn't breathe, and I was immediately overwhelmed by the terror of complete isolation. When Greg returned a little while later, he saw me smashing my arm cast against the side of the bed, my face twisted in fear, my eyes wide, my forehead wet with perspiration. For fifteen minutes I had been trying desperately to signal for help, but since my voice was still no more than a whisper I had no way of doing so. Greg thought he had never seen such absolute fear in a human being, had never witnessed so much frustration, despair, and pain in a person, all made so much worse because I had no power to cry out.

Once I calmed down, we talked about what had happened and realized that I needed to have extra help. Now that I was able to breathe on my own, I would no longer have a dedicated nurse. Alone for most of the night, I would be unable to speak, unable to pick up a call button, unable to call for assistance beyond banging on the metal bed rails. When I felt myself choking, no one would be there to provide immediate help. Strangely, though my recovery was proceeding well, my situation had abruptly become even more intolerable.

Fortunately Greg was able to find a solution to this problem the next day. At eight o'clock that evening, a Certified Nurse's Assistant named Kareen Brown came into my room and immediately set about making me comfortable. A large, handsome, dark-skinned woman from Jamaica who had an easy smile and a great laugh, Kareen remained by my side all that night. She suctioned the fluid from my mouth and throat, remade my bed, and gave me comfort. Most important, she completely vanquished my fear of isolation.

Kareen returned the following evening and soon became my constant nighttime companion. She would talk with me, tell me stories, and watch television with me. We especially enjoyed watching *Seinfeld* together; it felt good to laugh at those feckless characters. During those long nights in the Burn Center, Kareen—who ultimately worked with me for five years—helped create the first small bit of consistency in my life, so that it seemed a little more normal. Together we established a domestic cadence even in that most sterile and foreboding of places.

With the tube gone, I could at last begin to speak to those around me. My voice sounded pretty rough at first, and my nurses told me to take it easy. But it had been so long since I'd been able to talk, and I had so many questions. Within a couple of days, my throat was sore and scratchy from speaking so much.

I was especially eager to have conversations with the doctors, therapists, and nurses who had been caring for me for weeks. Dr. Yurt, the quarterback of my medical team, had been directing my treatment since my first moments at the Burn Center, but only now did we really come to know each other. We hit it off right away: Dr. Yurt was brilliant and funny, with a wicked sense of humor that matched my own. Among other things, I loved his aggressive approach to my care. My attitude was that together we would destroy any obstacle in my way. Our common enemy was anything that would prevent me from achieving a complete victory.

I also met and came to admire Dr. Lloyd Gayle, the soft-spoken plastic surgeon who helped me chart a long and complex course of treatment of scar releases and revisions. I got to know the elite group of therapists who had been working with me since long before I could work for myself: occupational therapist Robin Silver and physical therapists Hope Laznick, Tracy Maltz, Alyssa Padial, and others. And I became better acquainted with the nurses who had been responsible for my moment-to-moment care, including Andrew Greenway, the wild-eyed sentry who had announced my arrival on 8 West. Now that I was able to talk with him, I saw how thoughtful and humorous he was, and I came to feel tremendous appreciation for how much he and the other nurses—whom I had observed through an endless procession of twelve-hour shifts—were doing for me.

I was very clear in my mind that the ultimate responsibility for my recovery rested with me, and now that I was in a position to take charge, I planned to do exactly that. This was my body, and my life, and no one's desire to win this fight would be greater than my own. I also knew that the standards I set for myself would probably be higher than those set by my doctors and therapists, and that if I was extraordinarily dedicated to recovering, I could reasonably expect the same sort of dedication from them. I willed myself to win, and I willed my caregivers to join me rather than guide me.

Fortunately, everyone I was working with was a kindred spirit. The doctors, therapists, and nurses in 8 West were all trained to act quickly and decisively in an emergency, and they knew from long experience that there were no shortcuts to meaningful results. To the extent that I was willing to take the initiative, they were willing to help me, and this shared approach to the challenges I faced made my relationship with my medical team far stronger than it might have been otherwise. I was determined to work as hard as I possibly could, to meet every obstacle head-on, and to come up with a plan for meeting every challenge.

I was very conscientious about doing my facial exercises, as well as my arm and leg exercises. When Greg put music on, I would bob my head in an attempt to dance with him. But although I was glad to be making progress, I continued to be deeply concerned about my hands. I had received skin grafts to both hands in October, but otherwise they had been left to heal on their own.

As I entered the second half of November, my hands remained in their bandages and the prognosis for their recovery remained uncertain. Though Greg had continued to follow the Doppler readings, he had never raised the topic of my hands and fingers with me. For weeks, he had seen the black fingertips of my left hand poking through my bandages; he knew my doctors were waiting as long as possible before performing surgery on my hands, because once they intervened the limit of my healing would be reached. They had pinned my knuckle joints, but they wanted the soft tissue to heal as much as it could.

In late November, Dr. Yurt convened a planning meeting at my bedside, with Greg, my parents, and the social worker in attendance.

Looking at me, Dr. Yurt said, "It's good that we're having this meeting, because it means that you're getting out of this place."

I was scheduled to have my last surgery at the Burn Center the next day. During the operation, I would receive the final autografts to my right and left hands, and the doctors would also try to close an area on my buttocks that had so far refused to heal completely. Dr. Yurt told me and the others at my bedside that he expected that I would be released from the Burn Center in several weeks, and then the social worker discussed the various options among rehabilitation facilities.

That was the good news, but I also learned during this conversation that during the next day's surgery doctors would be removing the third segment of my index and middle fingers on my left hand, as well as a smaller amount from both my ring finger and pinkie. Parts of four fingers would be amputated. This was terribly disappointing: I was afraid that I might permanently lose the dexterity to do such things as holding a pencil or lifting a glass.

I remembered the night in college that a friend had lost a finger in a race to climb over the iron fence that ringed the campus. His finger got caught as he was descending, and he dangled from it like a rag doll before it gave way. My boyfriend ran over and picked the finger off the street; with a coolness that surprised even me, I took the finger from him, dropped it in a bag of ice, and then carried the bag as we raced from one hospital to another to find someone who could help. The finger was reattached, but in the days that followed it turned black, and finally it became obvious to us that he would lose it for good. Now, it was just as obvious to me that the black tips of my left hand's fingers had not survived; the only question was how much of the hand had healed enough to be saved.

"Why does the third piece have to be removed?" I asked.

Dr. Yurt explained that unless he amputated that segment, the finger might draw down into a claw tip, making it completely nonfunctional.

"All right," I said to Dr. Yurt, "but please make sure that whatever you do to my fingers looks as good as possible."

Then, after we discussed where the donor skin would be harvested from, the meeting appeared to be about to end. I turned toward the social worker to summarize what I had agreed to with respect to the likely rehabilitation centers. "Okay," I said, "so you'll apply to Burke and to Rusk." Then I looked at Dr. Yurt and said, "And you'll do the best job you can to fix me up." At that, my father delivered a dramatic salute, and everybody laughed.

I had just given everyone, including my surgeon, their marching orders. This was hardly the role typically played by a patient while lying in her bed, but I remained determined to be in charge of my own care. And because I was finally free of all narcotic medications, I signed my own surgical consent form for the first time, with Greg witnessing it.

The next morning Greg was at my side, as he had been for all my surgeries. As he walked beside my gurney to the elevator that would take me down to the operating room, he told me, one last time, that I would be fine.

"Pray for my hands," I said. "Pray that what they do looks good."

Greg responded, "I've been praying for your fingers since September 12."

The long weeks of healing had defined the areas of my hands and fingers that were viable, and now this final surgery would lock in their function. And with the skin grafts that would follow the surgery, the last 1½ percent of my body area would be covered. My immune system was at last growing stronger, and if these grafts held, I would finally be 100 percent closed.

After I came out of surgery and woke up, I was pleased to hear that the surgery had gone well. But I wanted to know more than that; I wanted to learn everything I could about how to achieve the best long-term outcome for my hands. I asked Dr. Yurt to bring in the best hand surgeon in the business for a consultation, and the next day I met with Dr. Andrew Weiland of the Hospital for Special Surgery. Dr. Weiland told me that although my right hand wasn't in great shape, it would be serviceable. As for my left hand, I would ultimately regain enough dexterity to grasp objects, write, and do much of what I wanted to do. But because of the extensive damage, I would never regain full function. Despite this mixed picture, Dr. Weiland's assessment was wonderful to hear. He and I agreed that we would have another consultation a month later.

What I didn't know then was that this wasn't the first time Dr. Weiland had evaluated me. Early in my stay at the Burn Center, while I was still sedated, Dr. Yurt had asked Dr. Weiland to advise him on how best to develop a splinting strategy that would preserve function in my hands. Dr. Weiland had examined my hands and made his recommendations, but he had come away from that visit believing that I wasn't going to live. When he saw me this time, he left with a completely different impression.

He thought I'd be fine.

———

Now that it was possible for me to have actual conversations, I wanted to know more about what had happened on 9/11. Greg, my parents, and my caregivers had been careful not to volunteer information about that day. They'd been advised to wait until I asked about it, and then to answer my questions without elaboration. That way, I could take in the information at my own pace.

Over the course of several conversations with Greg, I began to understand the enormity of the attacks. With my first question, I sought confirmation of what I had long since surmised.

"Was it an act of terror?"

"Yes," Greg replied.

I felt a deep sense of anguish, followed by a surge of anger. "I'm going to get those bastards," I whispered. Furious, I beat my forearm, still in its cast, against the bed.

"Lauren, you don't have to," Greg said. "The United States of America went to war. We are going to get these guys. And there are units over there who are fighting in honor of you."

Greg then told me about a letter he'd received from a helicopter pilot from the 106th Air Rescue Wing, which was based in Westhampton Beach on Long Island but had been deployed to Afghanistan. Greg read to me from the note. The pilot promised that he and his unit would deliver justice to the people who had launched the attacks. "We will not sleep and we will never go away," the note said. "These people will have to sleep with one eye open for the rest of their lives. We will do this in honor of Lauren."

The helicopter pilot also wrote that he had spoken with fighter pilots flying an F-15E, and with his note he included a photo of a missile hanging from the plane's undercarriage that had been inscribed "For: Lauren + Greg." Another photo showed that the pilots had written "Lauren's Sled" just below the cockpit window. The helicopter pilot informed us that the missile had been "delivered to the bad guys special delivery," and that we would soon receive an American flag that had been flown during the combat mission on October 21. Hearing that others had taken up the battle on our behalf told me that I was not alone in my fight.

My next question was about Cantor Fitzgerald. "Was anyone at Cantor hurt?" I asked.

"Yes," Greg said.

"Did people die?"

"Yes."

"Anyone I know?"

"I'm not sure," Greg answered. "Let's talk about that tomorrow. I have to check the list."

"Okay," I said, "I'll wait."

"But there is something you should know," Greg said. "You've become the hope for many families of the Cantor Fitzgerald victims, and you shouldn't see it as a burden, but as support. There are a lot of people praying for you.

"No matter what comes," he continued, "I'll be by your side, and we'll get through this. I'm going to take care of you, Lauren, and of Tyler." I nodded in assent, and then Greg paused for a moment. "Besides, we're probably one of the few couples who can say that following their engagement, each spouse had to relearn how to walk."

That line got a smile out of me, but otherwise I had little to feel good about. My newly recovered ability to speak inevitably led to conversations that only reminded me of where I was and how much healing I had left to do. In part because I was also learning what had happened on 9/11, I had been finding it very difficult to keep my spirits up.

———

The day after my first conversation with Greg about Cantor, I decided that I was ready to hear more. I had been with the company since 1993, and we had always been a very tight group. As a managing director, I knew all the other department heads and many of the people who worked for them, people from the top brokers to the security guards to the kitchen staff. I didn't know exactly what had happened to the company during and after the attack, but I knew it was terrible.

I began that second conversation by asking Greg whether Doug Gardner had survived. Doug, a tremendous person with whom I'd had an excellent working relationship, was Cantor's chief administrative officer.

"I'm not sure," Greg said. Then, after a pause, he continued. "No, I'll answer that one. He didn't make it." He paused again and said, "Are you okay?"

"I'm okay." I said. "I expected it. He was always at his desk by seven."

Next I asked him to get some things out of my office for me. He said he would, but I noticed that his manner was a bit awkward.

I asked a few other questions and then said, "How do the buildings look? Have they been dismantled?"

"Crews are working on them," Greg answered.

Returning to the topic of what had happened at Cantor, I asked about a number of other people from the company. Greg had brought in the list of names of those who had perished and those who had survived, and I was anxious to hear his answers.

"How is Joe Shea?" I asked. "Where is Don? What about Mark Colaio and Ian?" Greg patiently answered each of these questions by saying: "No, he didn't make it out." "No, she didn't either." "No, they didn't make it."

I asked about several others, including an assistant who had been pregnant. Greg told me that they had all died.

Finally, I looked at Greg. "How many died?" I asked.

"Do you really want to know?"

"Yes, I do."

Greg paused for a moment. "Almost seven hundred," he said.

I blinked. The number came as a tremendous shock, and I felt suffocated by the crushing news that so many had died. Yet I also felt rage at the terrorists for what they had done. I raised my right hand in its cast and spoke angrily through my tears.

"I will avenge them," I said.

Learning that hundreds from Cantor Fitzgerald had died that day was a devastating blow. Then I discovered that no one from any company who had been working above the ninetieth floor of the North Tower on 9/11 ever made it out. Finally Greg told me that I was one of just a handful of people who had been seriously injured that day and survived. Hearing this news, I experienced a profound and desperate sorrow.

Greg then went on to tell me the full breadth of what had happened: that the Pentagon had also been hit, that a fourth hijacked plane had crashed in Pennsylvania when passengers, who had heard about the other attacks when making calls on their cell phones, had attacked the terrorists and attempted to seize back control of the plane. I was astounded at the reach of the attacks and once again felt an enormous surge of anger. They had killed so many of my friends and so many others as well.

The terrorists came that day for the people who worked in the towers. The World Trade Center was filled with corporations, financial services companies, government offices, insurance companies; white- and blue-collar workers of many nationalities, ethnicities, and religions. The towers had stood as the ultimate collective symbol of American capitalism. But if the attackers' intention was to kill everyone in that building, I would make sure that in my case, they failed. At the very least, my survival would mean one fewer victory for the terrorists.

Now I had a new mission: I wanted to survive and prevail on behalf of all those who had died. I felt unconditional love for all of my coworkers. In many cases, I had known their families, their habits, their humor, and their work ethic. I knew their innocence. Most of all, I'd known the absolute terror they had felt that morning and the inescapable pain of their suffering. I was sure I'd known some of the people who had jumped from the towers to escape the flames.

I felt an upwelling of motivation, the boxer's refusal to go down easy. I vowed to put every ounce of effort I could into battling back. My family would be proud of me. My survival had given me a chance to make things right, to see beyond the small sorrows of everyday life.

I would not capitulate to the terrorists. I would not permit them to take one more moment from my life. Now I understood that I was indeed fighting a war while I lay there cloaked in bandages. My battlefield was the terrain of sterilized rooms and hushed voices, of surgical gowns and masks. My battle, though silent, was waged with the same ferocity as war. Some might look at me and see a profoundly injured person lying in a hospital bed; they might define me with a label such as *helpless woman, burn survivor*, or *terribly injured mom*. But those labels were all synonymous with *victim*, and I rejected that destiny. I detested the idea that someone might try to categorize me that way, framing my life through the prism of a single horrific day. I would not permit those cowards to define me. I would never surrender or hide; I would stand tall in this world.

Greg told me that the only battle I had to fight was my own, that I didn't need to be an avenging angel, just an angel of hope. As we talked, we agreed that all that really mattered was the home we were building for our family and the people we loved. Love defined everything we wanted to live for. From the first day I'd been injured, Greg had told me that I would be fine, and he had stayed by me and done everything he could to see that promise through. We had given each other our word and our vows, and we had honored them.

When I'd been sedated, Greg had sat beside me and read poetry, reaching out toward me when I could not reach out toward him. He had also told me stories, and one day he told me an especially elaborate one.

Before my injury, Greg had occasionally amused me with humorous tales about our relationship featuring a character he called the Princess of Perry Street; this time, he'd spun a story about a blond princess who lived in a city by the waters and journeyed daily to a castle with two towers where she did good works and was widely loved. One day, just as she entered the castle, two evil dragons descended on it and she was consumed by dragon's breath. The princess was put in a deep sleep and then brought back to life not only by her prince but also by her healers. And what brought her back were the love and prayers of the whole world, which were poured into the vessel of her prince and husband. Standing beside her, he laid his hand upon her and transferred all that love into her at each of the spots where she'd been hurt, until the princess had no more blood, but only pure love, coursing through her veins. And that love touched every part of her, in the depths of her sleep, from the inside out, and brought her back to her prince and their infant son.

Later, when my recovery was assured, Greg told me about the story and how he had held his hand over me as he spoke. He said he had never in his life willed anything more strongly than he had willed this story to be true.

Greg's mother, Liz Manning, survived the Holocaust. She witnessed the Anschluss and endured the violence of Kristallnacht. Hitler came to power as she was growing up, and as a slave laborer, and later an inmate at the concentration camp Terezin, she had survived Hitler's genocidal campaign against Europe's Jews. When she visited me in the hospital, she said, "I've seen many terrible things, but you have been through worse than me."

Her words reminded me that every generation has faced absolute terror, that there are people who have suffered as much as or more than me, who have endured the unendurable. As much as I'd like to believe that the future will be different, I can't convince myself that it will be. That, to me, is the awful truth of the primitive world we still live in.

Liz knew the face of hate: even before the Holocaust, she experienced the rising anger toward Jews, the invasion of Austria, the denigration of the Star of David. Yet throughout that dark time, she believed that it would pass, even though the unimaginable was becoming a stark reality before her eyes. Now, so many years later, we needed once again to convince ourselves that hate would not last forever.

Even before 9/11, I never questioned that absolute hate exists. But I had lived with a false sense of security and safety. The 1993 bombing of the World Trade Center, the 2000 bombing of the USS *Cole*, the suicide bombers in Israel—I was aware of all that, but remarkably I remained in a state of relative ignorance about the rising tide of fanaticism and the notion of jihad.

After the World Trade Center was bombed, my father said, "If you're going to be working in that place, you should have a gas mask." I remember laughing at his suggestion and saying, "Not to worry, Dad, this won't happen again. We have more police, security is much tighter, picture IDs are required, and the building is now surrounded by huge cylindrical cement planters."

But the truth was, we all knew the terrorists were coming back, and the emotional impact of that bombing was more powerful than any of my colleagues wanted to admit. We would make jokes about the next attack, but whenever there was a loud bang or the building shook for a moment or two, we would brace for what might happen next.

For years, we remained comfortable within our cocoon of ignorance, oblivious to the men who spent years devising a plot to kill as many of us as possible. But as I lay out on the berm on 9/11 in an agony of pain, looking up at the sky and its scar of black smoke, the one emotion I am sure I did not feel was surprise.

We knew they had returned.

But for all the hate that was unleashed on 9/11, there was an equal and opposite release of goodwill. As isolated as I was, I could feel it. While I fought my personal battle, I was hearing stories from the front, and they reminded me that although there is much evil in the world, there is also great goodness. I began to understand the state of the country and the tenor of the city, and I experienced directly the extraordinary generosity of people who reached out to help me and other survivors.

Nurses from all over the country came to assist the medical teams at Weill Cornell as part of the National Guard's Disaster Mobilization Assistance Team. The Guard deployed fifteen nurses in the Burn Center; at one point, my day nurse was from a burn unit in Minnesota, and my night nurse was from Boston. Later, I was honored to receive a patch from the MO-1 DMAT unit that sent four nurses to the Burn Center from September 29 to October 14, 2001, and to receive a memory book from them, which they titled "While You Were Sleeping."

The generosity of both friends and strangers amazed and humbled me. I couldn't have flowers or plants in my room, but I received innumerable cards, letters, blankets, quilts, balloons, and CDs. They were as varied as they were heartfelt. I received a quilt from a group of eleven- and twelve-year-old cross-country runners at an Ohio middle school, and a signed football jersey from the owner of an NFL team, who wrote that after reading the newspaper article about me, he wanted to send a jersey from "another Manning who likes to win." A woman named Sally Bauer sent me care packages every week; another woman wrote poetry for me every week. A man sent me special clasps so I could close my necklaces. One of my physical therapists, Tracy Maltz, ran the New York City Marathon wearing a T-Shirt saying, IN HONOR OF LAUREN MANNING, WTC SURVIVOR, and came back to tell me that she had felt me giving her wings.

Reflecting on this outpouring of support, I came to understand that what I thought of as my solitary battle wasn't solitary at all. So many people who had read the *New York Times* article or heard about my fight to survive seemed to be pulling for me.

Their encouragement was extraordinarily uplifting; it amazed me that people who didn't know me could possibly care so much about me. I felt that I had tapped into something universal, and I suddenly understood that we are all loved, that ultimately there is a divinity in humankind and an essential warmth we offer one another. I had somehow become a focus of this extraordinary energy, and through this communion with strangers, I felt touched by the hand of God.

I thought about these well-wishers often. In the immediate aftermath of 9/11, all the barriers we had erected between ourselves to protect and guarantee our privacy seemed to fall away. Our entire nation was traumatized; the injury felt like a wound to all Americans. That may explain why so many reached out to me, even if they didn't know me. People wanted to connect with someone who had been at the center of the tragedy, to do something to assist those who had been harmed. Many people volunteered their time and skill to help those in need after the attacks. By making that connection they helped heal others, even as they were healing themselves.

One of those volunteers, Christine Gordon, had recently spent a lot of time as a visitor in New York-Presbyterian after her boyfriend was struck by a car on the street. He had suffered numerous injuries and spent many weeks recuperating. Christine witnessed the tremendous effort that the doctors and nurses had devoted to his care, and she came away not only grateful for all they had done, but with a new appreciation of the level of commitment necessary to perform lifesaving work. Since the media had identified the Burn Center as the place where the greatest concentration of hypercritical patients had been taken, she knew that pressures on the medical staff would be enormous. Figuring that they would have little time to eat, Christine began showing up at the Burn Center with a team of unofficial volunteers and enough food to feed twenty or thirty people.

Three nights a week at six o'clock, Christine and her team would arrive with trays of food and set them down in the Burn Center's staff room for the medical team to enjoy. Ordinarily, the staff room was off-limits to patients and their families, but these were not normal times; just as the unit's doctors and nurses were working around the clock, so too were the patients' families waiting day and night, praying for miracles, sometimes simply hoping that their loved one would make it through another day. A week after Christine and her bounty of food first appeared, the medical staff began to invite the family members to join them for the nightly feast. Everyone would grab plates and then sit down together for a short while, eating and talking before the staff went back to work and the families returned to their anxious vigils. One night, Christine—who was a singer-songwriter by day—even brought in a Karaoke machine and performed a concert over dinner.

Greg met Christine during those very uncertain days when she took it upon herself to help feed everyone at the Burn Center and to bring the gift of music. They became fast friends, and Greg promised to introduce me to Christine when I was well enough.

For a long time, I had been completely indifferent to food. After I opened my eyes for the first time, what I most wanted was a drop of water or a piece of ice to cool my parched mouth. Like a traveler lost in the desert, I dreamed of drawing a cool draft of water. I dreamed it, wished it, obsessed over it. My lips were blistered and cracked, my mouth sticky like baked macadam on a hot summer's day. My throat and stomach were dry and barren. Most of the heat from my body seemed to be trapped inside my bandages, and I envisioned a long thin wisp of smoke escaping every time my lips parted. I imagined closing my teeth over the ice cube, hearing the slight scrape as it shifted and locked between my teeth, the muffled crackling and the small pieces shooting into the sides of my cheek, cold little surprises that would turn almost instantly into a welcome sliver of water sliding down my throat. I rolled my tongue around the imaginary cube, salivating at the thought of the cold delight.

In those first days of wakefulness, I was not allowed to have anything by mouth, not even water. The liquid diet still being pumped into me provided two thousand more calories per day than the bike riders in the Tour du France, who take in four thousand calories a day. This volume of nutrition was necessary during the most critical phase of my recovery, when the hyper-metabolic state brought severe risks of protein loss and muscle wasting at the very time my body needed to regenerate itself. But once my breathing tube was taken out, I received permission from Dr. Yurt to resume my epicurean life, albeit very slowly.

My first solid meal was a lavish menu of medium-sized ice cubes, clear and glassy, a maximum of three to an order. A broad, unwavering smile spread across my face; I was like a child tasting ice cream for the first time. The ice was delicious, and I took my time, savoring the broken chips as long as I could before they slipped down my throat. The second day the menu was more sophisticated: this time the ice was followed by a second course of Jell-O. When my dad pulled the foil off the top of the plastic container and proffered half a teaspoon of the beautiful, silky-smooth, jiggly-wiggly stuff, I felt as if I'd achieved nirvana. The raspberry flavor exploded in my mouth, liquefying and sliding over the outer edges of my tongue. That night I dreamed of Jell-O—yes, Jell-O.

Some people might have difficulty imagining how sweet that was, but believe me: it was a darn good dream.

On the third day, the culinary offerings became even more elaborate. I was given yogurt, applesauce, and more of my favorite, Jell-O. Even as I responded ecstatically to these delicacies, I had to chuckle at my obsession. Food had always been a joy and a blessing, but now I was reminded of how the very young and the very old often become preoccupied with their next meal. Even so, I savored every bite.

Since my days continued to be filled with therapies, biweekly graft surgeries, and the dreaded tank room for debridement of my wounds, food offered a respite from all that was painful and sad. I anxiously awaited my mom and dad's arrival in the morning; I looked forward to seeing them and talking at length about the day's lunch order. Food comforted all three of us; I knew that they were thrilled to see the progress I was making, but I also could sense that they remained anxious beneath calm veneers.

On the evening Christine Gordon first came to visit me in my room, she brought the gift of goodwill and Pasta Fagioli. Her long blond hair shimmered, and her eyes and face radiated a palpable energy. The scent of the soup was at first overwhelming. The distinct medicinal smells that had permeated my sterile room for weeks seemed to collide head-on with the earthy aroma of the peasant soup, but then the wonderful aroma of the soup got the upper hand. I was unable to feed myself, so Greg carefully lifted the spoon to my mouth, and with that first bite, I was hooked. The white beans and pasta—flavored with onions, garlic, oregano, and basil with a touch of Parmesan—were exquisite. The broth soothed my raw throat. The simple enjoyment of that meal and a friendship born of charity and caring stayed with me for years to come.

In the days that followed, eating good food would become an ecstatic sensory ritual. I remember the first sandwich in much the same way I recall my first kiss. Layers of tender spiced brisket, melted Swiss cheese, a touch of sauerkraut were all piled high atop a delicious marbled rye. It melted in my mouth.

Now that I was eating again, it was time to take on the next challenge. Dr. Yurt told me that I would have to get up and begin to move around or risk pneumonia. "Sure," I said with mock gravitas. "I can do that."

I will never forget the day I tried to sit up and stand for the first time. The room felt mighty crowded, with two physical therapists, a nurse, and my mom and dad attending me as I attempted this modest task. First I needed help just to sit up; the PTs gently took my legs, moved them toward the edge of my bed, and assisted me as I lowered my legs to the floor. As my legs moved over the side of the bed and down, the pain of putting weight on my legs for the first time in weeks was excruciating. My legs felt as if they were tearing apart.

We took a moment to prepare for the next stage, and then the PTs placed their hands under my elbows and across my back to aid me in standing. Sweat beaded on my forehead as I leaned my body forward and raised myself to a standing position. It was as if I were attempting a final lift at the end of a long workout: so much effort was required that my body was instantly fatigued, shaking with instability. My muscles were so depleted that they could barely maneuver my limbs through the smallest of movements. I stood, still shaking, but only for a second, before sagging into my therapists' arms.

I was shocked: I had no strength at all. It felt as if my legs were gone. I sat back down, weak with exhaustion. Tears welled in my eyes. I did not want to cry in front of all these people, but I could not use my hands so I couldn't wipe the tears away. Instead, I turned away, and as the PTs carefully swung my legs back onto the bed, a few tears dripped onto my gown.

For weeks I had been wearing pneumatic compression stockings over my legs as I lay in bed. Every minute or so, pressurized air was pumped into inflatable compartments in the stocking. Starting at my feet, the air moved up my legs like a wave, mimicking normal blood circulation and preventing blood clots from forming due to atrophy and lack of movement. Now, as I prepared not only to stand but to attempt to walk, the pneumatic stockings finally came off.

On November 12, I was ready to try standing and moving to a chair. My legs were like steel rods; though not particularly flexible, they transmitted pain very efficiently. I was prepared for my legs to collapse, and I willed power into them. When I began to stand I felt the spreading pain once again, but this time I slapped it down in my mind. The pain wanted to distract me, to make me fail, but I refused to let it. I willed my right leg to move. My ankles did not bend, but I was able to slide the right leg forward. I used this momentum to attempt the same with the left. This step was harder, the weakness and the pain were greater, but now I ruled the pain.

Sliding my legs slowly, one after the other, I moved all the way from the bed to the chair, where the PTs helped me slowly turn and sit down. I was so exhausted that without their help I would have collapsed into the chair face first. Once I was seated, the burning pain began radiating from my thighs upward. Even so, I was elated. On this Day of the Walking Mummy, as I came to call it, the thought of becoming ambulatory again was intoxicating.

My first physical milestones involved the simplest of activities, basic functions I had always taken for granted such as speaking, holding a fork to feed myself, sitting up, getting in and out of bed, and walking. Daily life waits for no one; the world rewards the healthy, and though it may care for the sick, it does not seek them out. Knowing that, I looked to my strengths. I rejoiced in the smallest accomplishments, and day-by-day I found my way forward through the many barriers and the detours in my path.

Every part of me seemed to be injured. My voice was very weak, and my throat hurt. The range of my voice was much lower than it had been, and a long time passed before it had any strength behind it.

Mastering the use of eating utensils was hard, but walking was especially difficult. My feet and ankles had been in splints, but I had not placed any weight on them for weeks. Because my muscles had atrophied and tightened, my feet and ankles had to remain in splints when I took my first tentative steps. I had to use a special walker, one with wheels and handbrakes, that carried some of the weight of my upper body and so gave my legs a chance to support me. Inevitably, I experienced occasional setbacks. In November, during a therapy session in the rehab gym, I fainted while trying to climb four simple steps. When I used my right hand to try to grab the stair rail, the pain caused me simply to black out. But going forward was the only way to get back.

I took painkillers every day—without them, I wouldn't have been able to go on. But I didn't like taking them and began to try to wean myself from them. Soon everything hurt, and Dr. Yurt became concerned about the level of pain I was experiencing.

When he asked me about it, I told him that I was attempting to cut down on the number of painkillers I was taking.

"Do you like feeling pain?" he asked.

"No."

"Then let us give you the medication that will control the pain so you can continue to heal."

I resumed taking the necessary medication, but I insisted on taking the lowest possible dose. The only thing I could do to exorcize my anguish and anger was to push myself even harder.

As the days passed I began spending a lot of time devising ways to beat my injuries. Pain was my opponent; I studied it and anticipated the ways it would try to take me down. At night after Greg had left and the nurses had finished their early rounds, I lay in the darkened room and thought about how I would meet the next challenge. Night sounds from elsewhere on the unit would occasionally drift in, but mostly it was quiet and I was free to think and develop a strategy for the next day. My game plan was always very tactical. Just as a coach and her team might review hours of tapes before game day, I would lie there and think, *How can I win tomorrow?*

As my energy returned, I realized that the do-or-die, eat-or-be-eaten attitude required in my job at Cantor Fitzgerald would be of great help to me now. I was used to pressure and unforgiving competition. There in the hospital, I turned that attitude to my advantage and used it to fuel my recovery. Some people say, "Oh, life's not always about winning and losing," but a lot of the time it pretty much is. Viewing my recovery as a win-or-lose situation was a productive way for me to approach painful procedures. The way I saw it, I had the enemy in my sights, and I wasn't going to show him any mercy. Every time I hurdled a new obstacle, I took it as a win, and every time I won a point my self-esteem improved. Much like a child, I was keeping score, using small achievements to build my confidence so that I could do even better the next time.

On November 15, I stood outside the door of my room, the therapists grasping each arm. The long hallway stretched out before me. My adrenaline surged. I took a step forward, and then another and another. I went past the next room and walked still farther down the hallway. As I hobbled forward, I thought, *I can do it and I will do it, I can do it and I will do it. Damn it, I will do it!* Over and over I chanted this mantra to myself. A group of therapists walked in front of me, and two peeled off and ran out to the waiting room to find my parents. I heard them say, "Run, come now, Lauren is walking!" Just as my mom and dad rushed back through the swinging doors, I reached the reception desk.

I had covered a distance of thirty to forty feet. My parents and therapists had tears in their eyes, as did others on the ward, but this time they were tears of happiness and surprise. Greg told me later that no one had expected me to walk that distance, or to walk at all, so soon after my injury. But I had done it, and from then on my mantra was always *I can do it and I will do it!*

6

HALFWAY HOME

Every parting is a form of death, as every reunion is a type of heaven.

—TRYON EDWARDS

It had been sixty-seven days since I had last seen my son. Even after emerging from the coma I had not recovered sufficiently for a visit; the risk of infection was simply too high. The only recent pictures I had of Tyler were those collected in a small photo album made for me after his first birthday party by one of the other moms. Whenever anyone came into my room, I encouraged them to look at the album, because I was so proud of my little boy. Those photos were my link to him, and I would often have my mom or my dad or Greg hold them for me so I could see him.

At last Dr. Yurt said it was safe for Tyler to visit, and on November 17 he was brought to the hospital for the first time. Because of the continuing risk of infection, Tyler and I would not be able to touch each other, but at least we could finally be in the same room. I was desperate to see him, but I was also afraid. I looked nothing at all like the mother who had kissed him good-bye on the morning of September 11. I was genuinely scared that Tyler wouldn't recognize me or would be afraid of me. I didn't share these thoughts with anyone as the day for his visit approached, worried that if I gave voice to them, my fears might become reality.

Though I was in much better shape than I had been, I was still far from a beauty queen. For our reunion I was seated in a vinyl-covered wheeled chair, swaddled in white bandages and sterile coverings from head to toe. Speaking remained difficult: unless someone pressed the patch on my tracheostomy hole, air bled out of the slit in my neck with a *whoosh* when I tried to say some-thing, and nothing came out of my mouth. I had very little hair, and since there was no need for Tyler to see my reddened, raw scalp, I wore a white Cantor Fitzgerald baseball cap with a navy blue insignia. On my lap was a dark blue shopping bag brimming with colored tissue paper; inside was a gift for him. I also wore a touch of perfume—on my clothing, not my skin—that I had sometimes worn in the past. I hoped that even if I proved virtu-ally unrecognizable to Tyler, he still might remember that fra-grance and so understand that beneath the sterile bandages and antiseptic salves was his mother.

My parents and my therapists and nurses worked hard to make the occasion as special as possible. The reunion would take place in the Quiet Room, a private space at the far end of the burn unit's main waiting area that was filled with toys and comfort-able furniture. Its purpose was to accommodate the often painful reunion of families, most importantly parents with their children. This was where I would face my fears of Tyler not remembering me or, worse, running from me in fear. As I waited with Greg to be brought out to see him, I felt like an expectant bride: I was overwhelmed with conflicting feelings of anticipation and worry.

"I get to see my baby after two months," I said to Greg. "I just can't wait to go down the hallway to see him."

At last everything was ready. The doors of 8 West opened before me, and my mother wheeled me outside the unit and turned right toward the waiting room. My heart raced with anxiety, and then, coming down the hall from the opposite direction, there was Tyler. My father had been waiting with him at the end of the hall, but Tyler had broken loose and started down the hallway himself. He was pushing a musical toy; tied to its handlebars was a red, heart-shaped balloon inscribed with I LOVE YOU.

"Hey, Greg, he's coming," my father said. My mother stopped pushing the wheelchair, and we waited for Tyler to reach us.

"Hi, hi," I said, as Tyler approached. He was wearing blue jeans and a blue-plaid flannel shirt with a corduroy collar; he looked so small in the wide hallway. The last time I had seen him he was a ten-and-a-half-month-old baby just beginning to stand in his crib. Three weeks past his first birthday, here he was, walking the length of the hallway toward me!

He arrived at my chair, stopped, and looked at me quizzically. My mother picked him up so he could see me better.

"That's Mommy," Greg said.

"That's your mommy," my father said behind him. "That's my little girl."

My mother continued to hold Tyler as Greg lifted the shopping bag off my lap and held it toward him, saying, "That's a little toy for you from Mommy, Tyler."

Tyler still seemed uncertain, but he wasn't afraid, and he was not turning away from me. I looked at him, rapt, swept away by emotion, and fighting back tears of happiness.

"It's wonderful seeing him, isn't it?" Greg said. I tried to speak, but the loose patch on my throat prevented me from making a sound, so I could only nod as Tyler smiled, playing with the balloon on its ribbon.

Together, we proceeded to the Quiet Room. Once inside, Greg held Tyler on his knee in front of me. Reaching toward the blankets on my lap, Tyler began to play with them.

"That's Mommy," my mother said. For the first time, Tyler looked directly at me and smiled. Finally, recognition filled his face: he knew it was me.

The first sight of Tyler coming down the hall had recalled the vision that had given me the strength to survive, but now his smile filled me with an even more powerful wave of emotion. My fears evaporated. My son and I had not been lost to each other.

"I love you," I said to him, my voice a raspy whisper. "I miss you."

Waving his arms up and down, Tyler made sounds that were a clear imitation of talk. Then, smiling again, he let go of the balloon and reached for the gift I'd brought for him, a white musical keyboard with animal-shaped keys. I had often sung a little tune for him, and now I sang it again. My voice was small and choked, but somehow I got all the way through it.

> I love you in the morning, and in the afternoon,
> I love you in the evening and underneath the moon.
> I love you, I love you, oh yes, oh yes I do.
> I love you oh my darling through and through.

Tyler played with the keyboard for a few moments and then decided he wanted to play with his push toy again. He was at the far end of the Quiet Room when my mother put his hands on the handlebars and said to him, "Go toward Mommy."

Tyler practically charged forward, taking three huge steps toward me with a beaming smile on his face.

Turning to Tyler, Greg said, "Where's Mommy?" Tyler pointed straight at me.

"That's right!" Greg said. "That's right!" He turned to me. "He knows who his mommy is."

My son still knew me. I could take a lifetime and still not find words enough to express how I felt at that moment.

Dr. Yurt appeared at the door in his white jacket and green scrubs, eager to meet Tyler.

"Say hello to Dr. Yurt," I said to Tyler. "He's helping me get better."

I could hardly take in how much our world had changed since I'd last seen my son. I sat in a vinyl rolling chair underneath layers of blankets. My face was bright red, my left ear mostly missing. I had only just begun to eat my first few bites of solid food, so a white feeding tube still ran up the front of me into my nose. Various bags of fluid hung from the side of my chair, and both my hands were encased in plaster splints. Even so, I'd been having a wonderful time.

Later, talking with Greg about the visit, I said, "This has been a watershed day in my life. Having my family around, especially my son, has been amazing. His voice, his running around, his smile—it's everything I fought to live for."

Even though I was in a wheelchair for Tyler's visit, we had both been rehearsing our first steps. With a little assistance from those we loved, we had learned how to stand up and how to walk. Now, at last, we could be together again.

On November 30, I announced to Greg, "The age of wireless has begun." Over the past few weeks, I had slowly begun reacquiring control over my body, and on that momentous day the last of the thicket of plastic tubes that had connected me to machines and measuring devices was finally removed. In seconds, I was on my own again.

Tyler paid his second visit to the hospital later that day, and for a while I sat in my rolling chair and watched him as he slept in his stroller. When he woke up, I leaned forward and kissed him. It was the first time I had touched him since September 11. All I could think of was how much I loved my little angel.

A few days later, I attended the meeting of a burn survivors support group. I told the group that I was glad to be alive and felt generally optimistic, although I was finding it hard to accept that the initial stages of my recovery would take not two months, but two years. To control the scarring, that was how long I would need to be vigilant about stretching, exercising, and wearing compression garments. Otherwise, the scars would form contractures, inflexible bands that might become yet another obstacle to reacquiring important ranges of motion.

During my last week at the Burn Center, I was measured for custom-fitting compression garments, and also for a clear, silicone-lined plastic mask that I would wear on my face almost constantly to control the scarring there. By now, I had begun an exercise program that involved twisting my torso and even spending a few minutes on a treadmill. But my hands would be the true challenge. Dr. Weiland had said that I could potentially recover a reasonable amount of dexterity, but it would take years of work to do so. I had already been given a mechanical device that would help each finger articulate its motions and splints that would hold my hands in various positions throughout the day.

Marking another milestone, I graduated from wearing hospital gowns to wearing gray hospital scrubs, both pants and a top. And for the first time since I'd been injured, Greg was able to gently massage my legs. For weeks I'd had needles and tubes put in me and taken out of me. I'd been poked and prodded and turned over. But now, finally, I felt the touch of gentle, loving hands.

Just before 8:00 p.m. on December 5, one of the nurses told Greg that a friend had come to the burn unit to drop something off for me. It was Gary Lambert, my colleague from Cantor Fitzgerald. He hadn't asked to come to my room, but I told Greg that I would see him. As Greg left to bring him in, Kareen, who had just arrived, made a fresh new bed and helped me get ready to receive my first nonfamily visitor since I'd opened my eyes.

Gary had worked with me at Cantor ever since I'd been asked to launch a new market data business. Now, dressed in the requisite gown, gloves, and surgical cap, Gary walked into my room. I said, "Hi," and then started to cry, thinking of all the others we had worked with who were gone. He was emotional too. I wanted to hug him, but I was still not strong enough to do that. Greg told Gary he could place his gloved hand on my forearm, and when Gary seemed unsure about doing so, Greg lifted his hand and placed it there. While we talked for the next hour or so, Gary never let go of my forearm.

"We lost so many friends," I said.

"So many," he said.

On the morning of September 11, Gary told me, he had just gotten off a bus on Vesey Street, a block from Tower One, when the first plane hit. If he'd arrived a few minutes earlier, he would have been upstairs in his office, and he would have died. That was the story for so many that day, and it was a common refrain for those who survived. *If I hadn't missed that train . . . If I hadn't stopped for coffee . . .*

We talked about all the work he was doing to execute the plan I'd had for the data business, and I was happy to hear that new people had joined Cantor to help the company begin to rebuild. Gary told me about all the people who had asked about me, which brought back a flood of memories. But speaking to him also reminded me that I wouldn't be leading the new data business, and though in the grand scheme of things it was a small thing to have lost, it still stung. I'd been so committed to my work for so long, and for now, at least, my career was another casualty of that awful day.

I told Gary how happy I was to be alive and then asked him to tell all those who had wished me well that I wouldn't let them down.

"Don't worry about any of that," Gary said. "You're alive, I'm alive. We have you—I have you, your family has you, Greg has you, Tyler has you. We all have you. That's all that matters."

For weeks I had been desperate to escape from the prison of my body's limitations, from the reminders of all that I had lost, from the small world of 8 West. I had not been outdoors for almost three months; I wanted to breathe fresh air, to feel the wind upon my face. Finally, on December 6, my nurses helped to bundle me up, and then Greg brought me downstairs in a wheelchair and wheeled me outside into a mild late-autumn afternoon.

The entrance to New York-Presbyterian Hospital is fronted by a circular cobblestone driveway with a grass-filled center island. People came and went, cars pulled in and out; all the sights and sounds seemed big and brash. I breathed in, and the air went down like a cool drink.

Sitting there with the sky above me, I understood that slowly I could begin to reenter the world. But as much as I wanted that, I was scared, too. I was so different now, and though the world hadn't changed, somehow it seemed brand-new. I had become accustomed to life in the Burn Center; knowing how much help I needed, I wasn't at all sure that I was ready to make the next move.

A scant fifteen minutes after going outside, I was chilled and ready to head back up. Feeling very tired, I said to Greg, "There's a whole world out there that I want to reconnect to. But I also realize how far I have to go."

On December 8, Howard stopped by to see me. I had been fully sedated the first time he'd visited, but now I smiled at him and said, "Check this out." Then I sat up, got out of bed, and stood on the floor.

"You're better," he said, grinning with pleasure. "This is a *lot* better."

We spoke about everyone who had been lost, including Howard's brother Gary, with whom I had been friends for eight years. I knew how much Howard was hurting. We talked for a long time, and he told me that it was a gift that I was alive, a gift to both Tyler and me that I would be there to share his life.

A few days before I was due to leave, Greg looked down at me and said, "You are amazing. You are so beautiful." I smiled, and he said, "You're my wife."

"Yeah, a wife who can't dress herself or feed herself."

"But you will."

"In a year."

"Well, we just have to gut it out. You have no idea how far you will go in the next year."

I told Greg that I loved him and we had to stay together. "We have to grow old and die together in a bed someday."

"Let's not rush that day," he said, "but yes, we will."

On December 12, Dr. Yurt came into my room to say goodbye. He said he would be happy to see my room empty, but sad to lose his sparring partner. I laughed, but then looked at him and said, "Thank you. Thank for saving my life."

Later that day, Dr. Yurt sent Greg an email: "At multidisciplinary rounds on Monday there was a spontaneous round of applause when it was announced that Lauren would be going to Burke the following day. I suppose that each member of the team was applauding each other. Thanks to your support and Lauren's fortitude, we are all proud."

Soon the EMTs who would give me my ride arrived, and Andrew Greenway, the same nurse who'd stood grim sentry the evening I arrived, signed my discharge papers with a big smile. I turned to Greg and said, "That's it. Ninety days to the day, and we're getting out of here."

And then I headed out of my room, down the hall, and, on my own, walked out of the doors of 8 West.

Just after noon, I arrived at Burke Rehabilitation Hospital in White Plains, New York, to begin the next stage of my transformation. My battle to survive was all but over, and though I took great satisfaction in my victory, I now faced a new challenge as I began to grapple with the infancy of my new life with a new body and a new face.

I felt like Alice in Wonderland taking a trip down the rabbit hole. The rhythms and routines at Weill Cornell had become entirely familiar, but now I encountered new people, new restrictions, and new challenges daily. I had emerged from the dark world of a coma and a burn unit only to be propelled into a parallel universe that bustled with activity and was governed by its own strict rules. I quickly understood that I would need to figure out how to operate successfully in this new world if I wanted to get back home.

After I checked in, a nurse brought Greg and me to a sad little room with drab, blue decor. (Months later I would learn that I was the last to endure its dreariness. The room was renovated shortly after my departure.) There was a separate bathroom with a toilet and a large shower that had grip bars and a call string in the event of an emergency. The sink, set in a three-foot-wide Formica counter, centered a vanity area in the main portion of the room. Above the sink was a mirror; soon after my arrival, I walked to the vanity, lifted my head up, and faced a full image of myself for the first time since 9/11.

My eyes looked just as they always had: blue, intense, and unflinching. But the rest of my face had the look of a fighter who caught the wrong side of a punch. My nose had been narrowed, the cartilage virtually collapsed on the outer areas of the nostrils. Drawing breath through my nostrils created a suction that further closed them, so I was forced to breathe through slightly parted lips. My mouth, meanwhile, pulled to the left, bound by thick scar tissue that ran from the midpoint of the left side of my neck up to my cheekbone. Two huge raised scars flanked my upper lips. The dimple in my chin had disappeared, along with most of my left ear.

Until that day, I really hadn't dealt with the way I looked. Now, staring back at me, I saw someone who was vaguely familiar. But as I looked at the poor woman in the mirror, I felt so sorry for her. A deep sadness overtook me, and quiet tears dripped down my face.

I turned to Greg and said, "I wish my tears could wash away my scars."

The mirror would remain my guide to the truth. I could not hide from it, nor would I.

My body, too, was terribly distorted. My back had taken the brunt of the hit. It was a craggy, distorted topography crisscrossed with roads that led nowhere. Graft lines cut through it haphazardly, evidence of the doctors' struggle to replace skin that was forever gone. Fortunately, I couldn't really see what my body looked like except in photos or a split look in a mirror. But I saw more than enough repulsive and tattered skin; I knew that much of my body had become a mottled tapestry of raised, hardened areas, the red and angry skin still in retreat from its initial thrust to heal.

I had come to terms with the negative feelings I'd had about my body when I was young, but the injuries I suffered on 9/11 resuscitated my unhealthy body image and my worst fears of inadequacy, and then slapped them down on the table in front of me like a dare. There was no escaping what had happened. I was boxed in on all sides, trapped. The only hope of release was to push through the pain and disfigurement. If I believed in my beauty and values, others would as well.

I quickly discovered that in the effort to accept my new body, optimism was an absolute necessity. I was able to keep a positive attitude partly by fooling myself. That injured person I saw in the mirror was not me but someone outside of me. I felt bad for that person—she had been so terribly hurt, she'd had to go through so much. But that was her, and I was me.

Now, like a good salesperson, I just needed to sell that idea to my toughest customer; I had to persuade myself to buy into the concept. It took an extraordinary leap for me to look down and release my being from the calamitous wreck of my body. I was not my old self any longer; anyone could see that.

The sense of dislocation I felt was exacerbated by the fact that I didn't see my body very often. I was covered either in bandages or in the flesh-colored pressure garments that encased my limbs. I got so used to wearing the garments that when I took them off I'd sometimes feel terribly disoriented; I experienced such a sense of otherness that it didn't seem possible that the body I was attached to could be mine. I also made a point of not looking at myself; only occasionally did I take a quick glimpse of my face in a mirror. I studiously avoided looking at my arms, and particularly my hands, when doctors examined me.

To some degree, then, my body was out of sight and almost out of mind. Looking back, I think my subconscious decided what I could and couldn't handle at different junctures. My brain somehow spared me the knowledge of my devastation and allowed me to focus on other things. It was as if my mind wore protective blinders and I, the horse, was rounding the turn, thoroughly in the moment yet separated from my situation. If I looked down and saw myself, I would fall and be trampled. It was far better to keep my distance from reality.

I was also aided by the positive attitudes around me. I chose to believe the doctors who assured me that my skin would improve. They were always there with comforting words: *you are doing better, great work, keep it up.* No doubt some of them were saying the

words just to say them. Even so, their assurances offered a wonderful ointment of hope. I believed them, and I learned to focus
on the positive reinforcement their words provided, something
I'd done far too infrequently in my past life.

It helped enormously that I was never alone in this parallel
universe. My health care aide, Kareen, remained my constant
companion from 8:00 p.m. to 8:00 a.m., often seven days a week.
Other aides, Lesma Williams and Louise Alexander, helped me
on those nights Kareen took off. I called Kareen Madame Curie
because of her healing presence; in response, she took to calling
me Madame Fury. I think she gave me that nickname because,
unlike some patients with catastrophic injuries who need to be
coaxed to engage in their therapy, I was motivated to do whatever I had to do to reclaim my life. But without Kareen's kindness, grace, and dedication, I would have had a very different
experience both at the hospital and at Burke. If I had been on my
own, I would have faced a lonely struggle to cope; instead, we
talked and laughed a lot as we went through my arduous routine.
For those difficult months, Kareen became like a second sister
to me.

When I arrived at Burke I was unable to feed myself—actually, I
was unable to move much at all. I couldn't dress myself, or clean
myself, or wipe away my own tears. I could not go to the bathroom
unassisted. I was unable to hold anything in my hand weighing
more than a few ounces or grip an object with enough consistent
pressure to hold it for more than ten to fifteen seconds. Virtually
every part of my body had been injured, so I would need to work
at my rehabilitation relentlessly and give it my continuous attention in the coming months. I kept my sanity by convincing myself

that if I took my therapy very seriously, so would others, which in the end would ensure that everything would work out.

I woke up every morning racked by pain and stiffness, unable to sit up. Kareen would change me, bathe me, brush my teeth for me, and feed me breakfast in my room. Then she would dress me and get me ready for "work." The whole process took at least an hour and a half.

Next I would head out of my room carrying a small canvas satchel that was filled with the resting splints I had worn overnight; they would be checked to see if they fit or needed to be recast. I had begun wearing the splints at the hospital to recover and maintain ranges of motion throughout my body, and I continued to wear them on my wrists and hands throughout my stay at Burke to preserve the accomplishments of my daily therapy. I thought of them as the business materials I brought to work each morning and came home with each evening. The hard part came at night, when Kareen put the current set of splints back on and so cranked me into my medieval torture chamber.

As I walked the hallways at Burke, I kind of shuffled along. I had developed a halting glide, a sort of drag walk. I couldn't raise either of my heels very far off the floor. My left foot was nearly immobile; it barely flexed at all, so I pulled it after me in an awkward version of Michael Jackson's moonwalk. Both ankles were covered with scar tissue that was very tender and would split open with any friction. The lack of flexion worked in my favor to a small degree, because when the skin on my feet did split, it was less liable to hurt since there was almost no friction against my shoes.

Meanwhile, my torso was twisted, and my left shoulder was raised and pulled up against my neck. I moved along pretty well, but I must have looked like a little old lady clutching her bag while trying to imitate the hunchback of Notre Dame.

The main elements of my program of therapy involved massage, which entailed a painful stretching of the newly grafted skin, exercise that restored strength to my atrophied muscle, and movement that further loosened the scar tissue to make it more pliable. The scarring that covered nearly the entire back of my body was roughly akin to an elastic band. Every movement stretched the minimal elasticity of my skin while the scar tissue pulled on itself, seeking to collapse back into its retracted form. And the pressure garments I wore were themselves elastic, so they applied a constant positive pressure to the surface of the scarring to keep it from thickening and contracting further. I felt like a caricature of a mummy come to life in some B-grade horror film.

After my morning bouts with occupational therapy I would return to my room and have lunch. Exhausted after three hours of active rehabilitation exercises, I would also take a nap. One way I marked my progress at Burke was by noting my improving eating and sleeping habits. At first, I ate all meals in my room and was fed from a tray; later, I ate breakfast and lunch by crudely managing to hold a spoon and shoveling in the food, Neanderthal-style, and then ate dinner after traveling all the way to the cafeteria. By my third month at Burke, I felt slightly less tired and so most days didn't take a nap during my lunch break before heading back to PT.

I considered my program of physical and occupational therapy to be my full-time job. I ran the operation seven days a week and threw myself into it with the single-mindedness I'd brought to my career for so many years. As I grew stronger, I came to know many of the other recovering patients at Burke. I would head down to the therapy rooms as if they were the practice fields, and once there I often gave words of encouragement to my fellow patients as if they were my teammates.

Here, at sixteen months, I'm playing with a push toy. Many years later, at a watershed moment in my life, my thirteen-month-old son would visit me while playing with a push toy of his own.

Greg and I on our wedding day, March 8, 2000. We were married at New York's City Hall; after a toast in front of the fountains in City Hall Park, we went back to work at the World Trade Center.

I had waited so long for a child and wanted it so much, and after our son was born in October 2000 I felt unbelievably lucky. Five months later, Greg, Tyler, and I visited my mom and dad on Skidaway Island in Georgia.

On November 17, 2001, more than two months after 9/11, I was finally allowed to see my son. I was afraid he wouldn't recognize me or, worse, that he'd be afraid of me. But my fears evaporated when his smile proved that we had not been lost to each other.

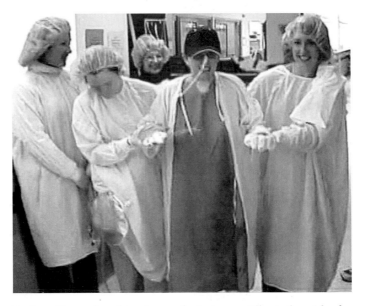

In late November I took my first steps without the aid of a walker. Here, I'm getting help from my sister Gigi (right) and one of my physical therapists, as my mom (rear) and sister-in-law Laura (left) look on.

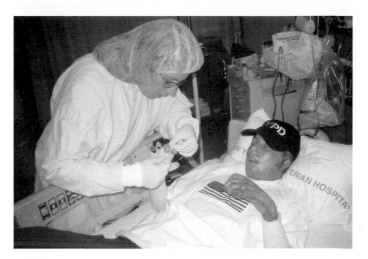

I was particularly concerned about whether I would ever regain the use of my hands, both of which were badly burned. Here, in late November 2001, Hope Laznick, assistant chief of physical therapy, is assisting me soon after surgery on my hands.

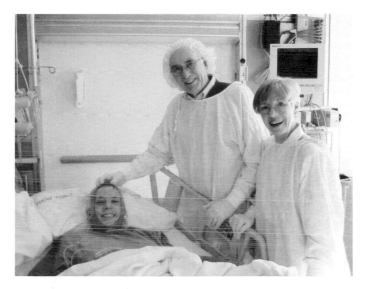

From the moment I opened my eyes, my mother and father became my partners in recovery, and they met every crisis with focus and determination. Here, in December 2001, near the end of my stay at Weill Cornell's William Randolph Hearst Burn Center, we enjoy a light moment.

In February 2002, Senator Hillary Rodham Clinton visited me at the Burke Rehabilitation Hospital in White Plains, NY. Our paths have crossed a number of times since that day, and she has always offered an embrace and an encouraging smile.

In May 2002, I got a welcome hug from Harry Waizer, an attorney at Cantor Fitzgerald who, like me, spent months at the Burn Center and at Burke recovering from his injuries. Behind us stood Howard Lutnick, Cantor Fitzgerald's CEO.

During my stay at Burke, Greg would bring Tyler to visit every weekend. Those forty-eight hours were the most anticipated part of the week for me. Seeing his face, holding him in my arms, kissing his soft, perfect skin—this was what I had lived for.

Librado Romero/The New York Times/Redux

I came to my physical and occupational therapy sessions at Burke tremendously damaged, but I was also very well-trained in the art of setting goals and fighting through obstacles to achieve them. Here, in March 2002, I am dancing with occupational therapist Rob Young.

Librado Romero/The New York Times/Redux

During my recovery, Greg told me, "No matter what comes, I'll be at your side, and we'll get through this." He would also say over and over, "You can go anywhere and do anything." The power and strength of that reassurance resonates with me still.

Certified nurse's assistant Kareen Brown, who first began working with me at the Burn Center, became a nearly constant companion for five years. Here, we share a happy moment in April 2002 soon after my return home.

On Mother's Day 2002, Greg, Tyler, my parents, and I visited the Central Park Zoo. I was very anxious about this public outing, but I focused on Tyler and lost myself in the moment.

Tyler's first day of nursery school in September 2003 was a big moment for both of us. I was so proud, but I was also worried about how his classmates and their parents would respond to me.

In June 2004, I was chosen to participate in the International Olympic Torch Relay in advance of the summer games in Athens. Here, Greg and I are running up Central Park West.

By the summer of 2004, I had come a long way. But when I look at this photo now, I see an injured stranger who had no idea how far she still had to go—a woman who, step by step, would become me.

Two sisters, side by side. The great distance between the paths Gigi and I had followed could have separated us forever, but instead we became much closer during my recovery. Here, we smile for Greg's camera in October 2008.

In July 2009, Greg and I decided to take Tyler on a grand adventure and then deliver a piece of very happy news. Here, at the Trevi Fountain in Rome, Tyler learns that a baby brother is on the way.

Thanks to an extraordinary woman named Juliet Jones, who became our gestational carrier, Greg and I were able to have a second child. Here, in October 2009, Greg holds three-day-old Jagger while Juliet and I beam with pride.

On Father's Day 2010, the four of us visited the Central Park Zoo. This time, I didn't have to wear sun-protective clothing or a broad-brimmed hat. When I look at my family now, I see everything I ever dreamed of.

My doctor at Burke, Richard Novitch, had initially expressed concern that I might be receiving more therapy than I could tolerate. I was carrying a quadruple load; I had double or triple sessions of OT in the morning and double or triple sessions of PT in the afternoon. Dr. Novitch told me I was getting more therapy than anyone at Burke had ever had.

But I trusted myself to know my limits, and I wanted as much therapy as I could possibly bear. I knew that I had a limited amount of time to get my life back, because there's a fairly brief period within which the bulk of scar maturation occurs. Typically burn patients have twelve to fifteen months to get the maximum amount of function back, although occupational therapy benefits the hands for one to two years. But as time goes on and both skin and muscles heal, they tighten and contract, and patients who haven't kept pushing through the pain can find themselves immobilized.

Having been burned over more than 80 percent of my body, I understood early on that unless I did the requisite therapy, I'd be compromised for the rest of my life. Or, to put it more bluntly, I knew that if I didn't push myself to the absolute limit of my endurance, I would eventually turn into a wooden soldier. That was all the motivation I needed.

While at Burke, I was privileged to meet and work with some of the most skilled and dedicated OTs and PTs in the field. Four of them in particular were so terrific that we have remained in touch all these years later: Rob Young, Tina Forenz, Liz Malon, and Corina Hall.

Rob continued the aggressive manual therapy I'd been receiving, and early in my treatment I would shudder from the pain it caused. But eventually I learned to manage the pain with

a combination of medication, controlled breathing, and medita-
tion. Humor also offered a wonderful distraction.

"Your joints are like the creaky doors at a haunted house," Rob
would joke.

"Yes," I would reply, "and yours will be too after you're done
working with me."

Tina, who was also assigned to my treatment because of the
unusual amount of OT I needed, collaborated particularly closely
with Rob and me. Over the next three months the three of us spent
so much time together that our relationship became an important
part of my therapy. We shared much laughter and many tears,
sometimes in the same session.

Rob, Tina, and the other OTs and PTs consistently rose to the
occasion. They promised they would help me pick up my pieces
and put my body together again. That was all I wanted, and we
made an incredibly cohesive team.

I had come to OT tremendously damaged, but also well trained
in the art of setting goals and fighting through obstacles to
achieve them. Again I drew on my experience in the competitive
environment on Wall Street, where I had thrived on the pressure
that accompanied the push to complete a difficult project. I took
particular pleasure in building teams of people and seeing each
member contribute their best work. It was tremendously satisfying to collaborate with motivated people who had a clear sense of
where they were going and would make the necessary sacrifices
to get there. Before September 11 these challenges had been professional. But from the moment I was injured, the challenges I
faced became deeply personal, and the stakes were immeasurably
higher.

I was a prisoner in my own body, but I didn't accept that as
my fate. It wouldn't be enough just to survive—I wanted my life

back. I wanted the independence that I'd always taken for granted; I wanted to be able to do all the things I had done before. I wanted to type, dial a phone, drive a car, swing a golf club. I wanted to pick up and hold my son.

My OTs and PTs began my therapy at Burke by saying, "You can do it," and I can't possibly convey the power of those simple words. More than reassurance, they helped me to see past the pain, to believe in a future. I needed to be set free, and through shared, focused effort, I would be.

As my recovery proceeded and my body healed, my mind became stronger as well. I saw my situation clearly now: it would take years for me to reach my goal of living something like a normal life again. Even then, it wasn't clear how far I could go. My doctors had told me, for instance, that I would have function in my hands, but it was still to be determined exactly what that meant. What I did know was that I would do whatever it took to achieve the best possible outcome. As Winston Churchill once said, "I have nothing to offer but blood, toil, tears and sweat."

I approached the process of reconstructing my life much as a builder would. Key to my success was a strong foundation, and my plan was to take all the blessings of medical care, love, and prayer and use them as the base for everything I built. Also crucial was my integrity and personal commitment. I felt a deep sense of duty and honor to do my best, and knowing that I had made every possible effort to succeed would allow me to feel enormous contentment. As I faced my future, I now felt utterly calm and determined.

Of course, no one would be happy to be in my situation. I was separated from my family and my life; my body had permanently changed; I remained in deep mourning for all of my friends and colleagues who had lost their lives. And plenty of "if-only's" ran through my head. I would think about the dark gray-blue suit I wore on 9/11, the one with pants, jacket, and a camisole. It was just a thin suit, a lightweight thing, and silk is a combustible material. I would sometimes think, *Damn, if only it had been a different time of year, I'd have been able to get the fire out sooner. What if it had been winter and I'd been wearing boots and a heavy coat? How different the outcome might have been . . .*

But I was also able, very early on, to assess how fortunate I was in so many ways. Even while still in the hospital I had said to myself, *Okay, I've just been dealt a hand. My body is profoundly damaged, but consider all my good fortune. I am alive, I have my family, I have my husband. After all, he too should have died. It is a true miracle that my son isn't an orphan.*

Part of my good luck was that I knew who I was. Even in the worst moments, I never lost my sense of my own identity. God asks us first and foremost to love ourselves, and I believe that this is one of the secrets to being productive in life. When a tragedy befalls you and your identity is ripped away, emotionally and physically, you may be petrified about what's next simply because you don't know what it is to meet yourself, you don't know who you are, or you are afraid to embrace that self. But when you truly respect yourself, when you deeply believe in the value of your soul, you will always survive. And somehow—tatters and all, imperfect as ever—I was able to believe in my own worth and commit myself to living a full life again.

My father was a marine, and he had a very simple motto: *Get over it.* From the time I was about nine or ten, no matter what happened, that simple message resonated with me. Life is full of unfortunate events, after all, and now I had to square my shoulders, look my bad luck straight in the eye, and get over it. I believed that the pain wouldn't last forever and that my battered body was best served by simply moving forward. My internal resolve never wavered; deep in my bones, I truly believed that I would indeed be okay.

During my time at Burke, Greg and I would often have a version of the same conversation. I would say to him, "I don't know if I will ever feel the same as I did before, but I am going to pull myself out of this hole, and there is no reason why I shouldn't look the best I can doing it." In response, Greg would say, "You can go anywhere and do anything, Lauren, and you'll be fine." Like a prayer, he would say those words over and over, and their echo and strength resonate with me still.

Feeling good about my looks, however, was a distinct challenge. My face was swollen and lined with bright red ridges. I wore a custom-fitted silicone mask that was attached with braces around my head. It covered my entire face save the eyes and nostrils, and a small hole was cut for my mouth. My entire body was still sheathed in Jobst garments. I lived inside a straitjacket of tight fabric and silicone; my only relief from this chamber of horrors came when I showered or received a massage.

Not until I'd been at Burke for two months did I receive my first set of custom-fitted garments; in the interim, I wore used garments that the hospital had given me. None of them were quite tight enough, but I didn't mind. The wound in my left arm and hand was so deep and still so inflamed that I was unable to bear the compression without feeling dizzy.

During a fitting I once asked a representative from Jobst if people wore these sorts of garments after liposuction. She told me that the materials were the same, but the compression and torque of the fabric on the body were on a completely different level. *Good,* I thought to myself, *I want as much pain as I can stand.* Pain had been my enemy, but after so much time in its company, I recruited it to be my ally.

Burke became our dorm, our barracks. Flanking me on the right and left were my fellow 9/11 survivors, three people who had also escaped the World Trade Center, survived with severe burns, and now faced many of the same challenges I did. Harry Waizer was down the hall, and Donovan, a young guy just starting out in his career, who was at Burke for only a few weeks, lived on the corner. Elaine, who worked for the Port Authority, resided in the room next to mine, the last of us to arrive. We were hardly a merry bunch, but we were in it together.

We would see one another in OT and PT throughout the day and then pay visits to each other in the evenings. At night I would often stop by Donovan's room to say hello or spend a few minutes chatting with Elaine. I regularly walked down the hall to see Harry, whose wife, Karen, and one or more of his three children were a daily presence at Burke.

One evening I was given special permission to leave the premises. Harry and I both celebrated February birthdays, and it was a great occasion when Karen hosted a small birthday party for Harry and me at their home. This would be one of my first forays out of Burke and into the real world. Greg and Tyler came too, and together we all sat around Harry and Karen's dining room table, which was covered with plates and bowls of delicious, steaming food. After five months, it was slightly disconcerting for me not to be in an institutional environment, but the smell of Karen's wonderful home-cooked food and the warm, comfortable surroundings were a welcome sensual and psychological relief. Tyler sat to my left in a high chair, and when the room darkened, he tried to sing along with the birthday song. After Harry and I blew out our candles, Tyler clapped his hands and leaned over to hug me. That simple birthday celebration remains one of my fondest memories.

As everyone's recovery progressed, word began to circulate about potential release dates. Donovan was the first to go, and then Harry was given his date. The day Harry left was especially sad for me. When I passed his room, my eyes would fill with tears. We had been together on this journey for many weeks, regaling each other with stories about our trials and setbacks. Now he was home, and I was so happy for him. But like a sick child who isn't allowed to go outside to play with her friends, I felt alone and left behind once again.

As for my release date from Burke, I was told only, "We'll see, Lauren. Not yet." I was disappointed—I had been working so hard. But given the severity of my injury, it wasn't surprising that I wasn't ready to go home. Dr. Novitch said I needed to be patient, but he also told me that because I was so highly motivated, I would be released from Burke far sooner than I might have been.

When I first arrived at Burke, I decided that if I had to live in that bleak little room, I would at least find a way to improve it. I made a series of requests for plants, furniture, and wall hangings. My room might never be a designer showcase, but it could be made more habitable.

As part of this effort, Greg brought me a small tabletop set of drawers where I could keep some personal items and display family photos and get-well memorabilia. Gigi made my room immeasurably warmer by hanging cards and posters on the walls. Gifts from all sorts of people, both friends and strangers, adorned the windowsill, bureau, and table. Among these was a white teddy bear with gold wings from the Salvation Army. I kept it in a prominent position on the table because it was one of Tyler's favorite weekend playthings.

One afternoon I came back to my room and noticed that the little white bear was lying on the floor. I decided that I would pick it up myself, and so began to reach for it. I bent down, leaning forward to the limits of my range. I was able to reach just far enough to touch the tips of my fingers to the tip of the golden wings, but then my crippled body behaved like a tightly wound spring and yanked me back up. I tried again, and the same thing happened. After a third failed attempt, I began feeling a bit like a yo-yo on a string.

Bending down with no assistance required an enormous amount of exertion. I couldn't get much closer than a few inches from the floor, and then only for a few seconds at a time. But with the bear lying on his back, those golden wings were pointing up and just within my reach. My fingers brushed against the tips of the wings a number of times, but the bear kept narrowly evading my grip. I felt like I was bobbing for the world's most elusive apple.

"I am going to get you, bear—I'm going to get you this time," I said aloud. Reaching down, I squeezed the tips of my right index and middle fingers together as tightly as I could, trying to use them like a lobster's pincer. Finally, miraculously, I got a firm hold on one of the small wings. At last he was mine! The little bear rose up in my fingers, and I rotated my shoulder, my arm extending like a steam shovel over the bed, where I released my grip. The bear was off the floor!

I exhaled, feeling both exhausted and thrilled. It had taken me about half an hour, but I had done it, and now I had exciting news to share with Greg that night. Silly as it sounds, picking that bear up off the floor was a huge moment for me. And the following weekend, Greg and I got a big laugh when we placed toys and animals—including the bear—on a chair so that Tyler could easily reach them. At one point, he spotted the little bear, plucked it up by the wings, and promptly dropped it back on the floor, oblivious to its significance. He was ready to move on to something new.

During my stay at Burke, Greg would bring Tyler to visit every weekend. Those forty-eight hours were the most anticipated part of the week for me.

When Tyler was born, my days suddenly slowed and stretched. For the first few weeks of his life, time seemed limitless. There would always be a new day, a new milestone, and there was always another special moment just around the corner. The immediacy of those early days eventually yielded to the rapid rhythms of daily life, but the notion that I would always be there with him remained. After 9/11, my perspective changed dramatically. When you believe that nothing can possibly go wrong, you don't treasure the little moments because you expect there will always be more. Having nearly lost all the moments of my son's life, I now realized how important each of those early days really had been.

On Saturdays and Sundays, the faster pace typical of the weekdays—the chatter of aides and nurses, the voices of patients calling out to one another—fell away. Like an expectant child I would sit in my room, listening for footsteps and the sound of the stroller wheeling across the linoleum floors, waiting for my world to flood with Tyler's squealing laughter.

Sometimes I worried that when Tyler came to visit he would witness things that most young children never have to see. Burke was full of people who were injured and badly impaired, and during some of his visits I was suffering terribly. But I believed that not seeing or having contact with his mother for so many of his early, formative months would be equally damaging. Besides, as soon as he arrived all my worries fled. Tyler was clearly fascinated by the medical equipment and entertained by the attention of the hospital staff; most of all, he was obviously very happy to see me. We were together, and that was all that mattered.

We took many happy walks down the halls, and of course I was always proud to show Tyler off. I beamed when I saw the eagerness for life that emanated from this unmarred extension of me. Soon everyone knew Tyler, and he became the miniature mayor, toddling down corridors, peering in rooms. He brought the gift of innocence and happiness to all who came in contact with him.

He especially enjoyed visiting the occupational and physical therapy gyms, each of which was more than a hundred feet long. Both gyms were flanked by a wall of east-facing windows on one side and private treatment rooms on the other. These rooms were filled with treatment tables, all sorts of exercise equipment, assorted odd objects, and colorful collections of exercise balls in all different sizes. The treatment rooms became his playground, and in no time he learned how to dribble a large exercise ball, skillfully bouncing it with his right hand.

Our walks became steadily longer as Tyler grew and became more confident. Similarly, the hitches in my gait changed and diminished as I continued to heal. With greater flexibility and strength in my ankles, my motions became more normal. During my weekly evaluation walk with Liz Malon, one of my PTs, I made it a point to move as strongly and decisively as possible to show how much progress I was making. Six weeks after my arrival at Burke, I was told that we didn't need to take that walk anymore.

Those weekend visits with Tyler meant the world to me. Seeing his face, holding him in my arms, kissing his soft, perfect skin— this, after all, was what I had lived for. But as much as I loved walking through the hallways at Burke with Tyler, I yearned to be home with him. Before too much longer, I promised myself, we would be together every day. And one fine morning, I would get down on the floor with him and take him in my arms. We would roll, we would play, we would laugh and be silly just like any other mother and her child

Before 9/11, Greg and I had worked long hours and spent virtually all of our free time with Tyler. We almost never went out, and a night at the movies was practically unheard of. So when the staff at Burke announced a movie night, one that would involve a trip to the local Cineplex, Greg suggested that we sign up. It was an opportunity to do something different, but it was also a way for me to achieve a new milestone. The program at Burke is goal-oriented, and it's designed to help patients reintegrate into the environment around them and gradually resume the tasks of daily living. But since this would be my first public outing, I felt a lot of trepidation. My injury couldn't be hidden, and the thought of being observed by strangers made me feel weak and self-conscious.

One night in late February, a group of patients, along with several family members, gathered at Burke's main entrance. Those who could walk boarded the handicapped van, and we were soon joined by several patients in wheelchairs who were moved into the vehicle with a hydraulic lift. We were driven to the movie theater, and once we arrived we disembarked in the handicapped area outside the theater doors.

Other moviegoers filed past. Many glanced at us, and most tried to be discreet while observing us. The therapists helped unload everyone from the bus and pushed the wheelchairs up the sidewalk ramp. Greg and I asked if we could help, but we were told that our assistance wasn't needed. Just then, a group of teenagers sauntered by; staring at us, they nudged each other and snickered. Seeing them, I immediately turned and placed my hands on the handles of a nearby wheelchair. Then, using my body weight for leverage and my hands as mere place holders, I safely moved an elderly woman up the small ramp. I turned to help another, wanting to do everything possible to avoid being seen as handicapped. If I appeared to be doing something useful, perhaps I wouldn't be perceived as a citizen of the disabled world. Of course, it was obvious to any observer that I belonged in that group, but this was my way to take a few steps outside of the world I had been cast into.

Once inside the theater, I was beset by the brightness of the lights around the concession stand and the cloyingly sweet smell of melted butter and cheese. For nearly half a year I had lived in places that were painted in blandly neutral colors: whites and off-whites, creamy beiges and taupes, occasional accents of gray here and there. Now, the garish display cases featuring countless brightly colored boxes and packages of candy and chips swirled in front of me. Beneath my feet, the Paul Smith–inspired wave of carpet seemed to pitch and roll. As music blared in the background, I began to feel dizzy and told Greg that I needed to sit down.

Together, we moved into the theater and walked toward a special area that accommodated wheelchairs. At the end of the handicapped row, there were a few seats with extra legroom, and that was where Greg and I settled.

The movie we saw that night was *Ocean's Eleven*. Right from the beginning, I felt bombarded by its fast-changing visuals, saturated colors, and loud soundtrack. My senses were overwhelmed. At one point I looked around and realized that I was indeed different. Though I was taking part in an ordinary activity, I couldn't respond in the usual way. Sensing my anxiety, Greg protectively put his arm around me and kissed my forehead. Then he gently took my hand.

I wore a bulky glove filled with hardened silicone inserts that separated the webbing between my fingers. When Greg applied the slightest bit of pressure, the hypersensitivity of my skin and damaged hand felt it immediately. I wanted to pull away, but instead I pushed my hand forward through his grasp so that his hand now rested on my wrist and forearm. Gradually the pain subsided.

As the movie went on, my attention drifted. The sounds and stimuli were too much, too loud. Finally, wishing it would end, I closed my eyes. And when the movie was over, I was relieved. Now I could go home to Burke, back to my quiet room and my predictable world.

When Greg and Tyler left on Sundays, I'd listen to the tenor of their voices as they trailed away, turned the far corner of the hall, and were gone. Alone again, I felt a tremendous separation, punctuated by the sudden and eerie quiet. Memories of what had happened and the reality of my new world were no longer restrained by the presence of my family, and deep heaving sighs of sadness sputtered up and out of me at the loss of so much and so many.

Eventually, though, my spirits would rise again. I was especially excited whenever I had a chance for a couple hours' parole from the Big House in the company of my therapists. Once we went out for pizza, and another time we drove to Dunkin' Donuts to get coffee and doughnuts for the group. Physically, these trips were difficult for me, but they were laced with the happiness of slowly becoming a part of ordinary life once again.

I'll never forget the first day I went to Bloomingdale's with my therapists to buy makeup. It was such a simple thing, but walking through a big department store and standing at the cosmetics counter made me feel as if I'd rejoined the world. Later, after returning to Burke, I stood before the mirror with trepidation and resolve. An aide had opened the lid of an eye shadow compact for me. My hands shook as I lifted the applicator; poking it through the eyehole in my mask, I crudely applied a dash of color to my eyelid. I thought back to the day when, as a young teen, I had put on eye shadow for the first time. My face was new to me then; now, it was new to me again. This would be the face I would live with for the rest of my life.

Toward the end of February, I was particularly cheered by several visits. Senator Hillary Clinton had sent me an encouraging note back in October, and it happened that one of Harry's neighbors, Geri Shapiro, was Senator Clinton's Westchester County coordinator. Now Geri was making arrangements for the senator to visit Burke, and I was told she wanted to meet me.

I didn't know what to expect from her visit, and in any case I was somewhat distracted that day because I was once again preoccupied with the condition of my left hand. I had recently lost another stabilizing pin from one of my finger joints, and I was very concerned that I wouldn't be able to pick up and hold on to the small blocks that I would be asked to stack during the following day's occupational therapy session.

When Senator Clinton arrived, I was struck by her beautiful blue eyes, which radiated a kindness and strength that immediately put me at ease. She had a ready, open smile, and I was impressed by her obvious intelligence and warmth. She seemed sincerely committed to helping us, and I felt sure that to her I was neither a statistic nor an opportunity.

After greeting me, she gently hugged me. Then she sat down and did what most people don't do well: she listened, as I asked that she be there for those of us who were known as the catastrophically injured. Her visit meant a great deal to me, and since that day our paths have crossed many times. She has always offered an embrace and an encouraging smile.

Another welcome visitor was Greg's dad, Bert. Then eighty-one and still going strong, Bert spent two months every winter skiing at Belleayre Mountain in the Catskills. Twice a week, he would drive down to Burke in his big Pontiac Bonneville and keep me company for a while. But one Saturday in February, he had an accident on his way to see me; after skidding on a curve, he careened into a guardrail. He suffered enough bumps and bruises to merit a hospital visit, but he kept to his appointed round. During our visit he never complained about it; instead, he was only interested in how I was doing.

One of the most surprising visits I received that month was from an old friend named Kerri Topping. I met Kerri in 1993 on my first day at Cantor Fitzgerald. A beautiful woman with green eyes and dark hair, Kerri made me feel instantly welcome at the company. I liked her right away: she had a gentle manner, respected the feelings of others, and was naturally self-deprecating. She could also make me laugh, and within a very short time she and I became fast friends. We became Betty and Veronica, spending much of our workday together and embarking on serial adventures after work.

Kerri and I bonded over so many things. Our sense of humor was the same; conversations were always easy and fun, and we'd end up laughing till we cried. When we really needed help or support, we were there for each other. But a couple of years later, when I moved to MDC, Kerri made a career change and our friendship fell away.

I felt I had lost my soul sister. Years passed, and one day I ran across her wedding announcement in the *New York Times*. It was devastating to know that I hadn't been part of that special day for my onetime best friend. But after 9/11, Kerri got in touch with Greg and told him that she wanted to see me. When Greg showed me her e-mail, I was stunned and elated, and when she came to visit me at Burke, it was as if our friendship had never ended. I hadn't seen her in five and a half years, yet here she was, as wonderful and warm and loving as ever. She brought her husband, David, and a gift basket full of treats, but what really mattered was seeing her again. After that day, our friendship resumed in full force, and even now we frequently comment on what a joy it is to have each other back.

Other long-lost friends have also come back into my life since 9/11. Like so many others, I had let a number of important friendships lapse as I increasingly socialized with colleagues from work or people who lived nearby. My renewed friendship with Kerri, as well as the return of others with whom I had once been close, provided an important reminder that unless we really make the effort, friends can drift away. For all the pain and hardship that 9/11 brought into my life, for all the people I lost, I'm grateful that so many old friends were found.

One evening in March, I was given another special dispensation to leave the premises for a few hours. The Woman's Bond Club, a network of experienced professional women from the capital markets industry, had chosen to honor me at its annual gala event. Despite my frail condition, I looked forward to going into the city and seeing a room full of friends and colleagues.

Greg and I drove into the city just after dark, and as we proceeded down the West Side Highway, I looked south and saw two white beacons rising thousands of feet into the black sky. At first I was mystified, but then I realized that the powerful beams of light were shooting upward from the empty footprint of the World Trade Center. Mesmerized by the void and by the light, I imagined that the beacons lifted up the spirits of those who were gone, their intensity and brilliance piercing the dark night sky.

7

HOMECOMING

I love you—I am at rest with you—I have come home.

—DOROTHY L. SAYERS

At 8:30 a.m. on Tuesday, September 11, 2001, I left for work. At 11:45 a.m. on Friday, March 15, 2002—six months and four days later—I finally returned home.

Earlier in the week, my friends at Burke had thrown a good-bye party for me. The nurses and my physical and occupational therapists, as well as many of the other patients, gathered to wish me well. There were lovely gifts and tremendous hugs and more than a few tears. I was excited to be leaving Burke; going home to my family had been my greatest goal. But in an odd way, I was slightly sad—and a little afraid.

Burke had been my home, however involuntarily. I knew many of the employees and many of my fellow patients. I knew the building intimately. I had adapted to its rhythms and found comfort in its hallways and treatment rooms. My rehabilitation had provided a necessary focus for my energy; by becoming an all-consuming job, it had kept at bay the extraordinary sadness I felt at the loss of so many people who had been a part of my daily life.

Now that it was time to leave, I realized how much I would miss Rob, Tina, Corina, Liz, and the many others who had done so much to help and inspire me during my recovery.

Though I was grateful for all the support I'd received throughout my time at Burke, I had often sought out spots in the greenhouse and library and visiting room where I could be alone and so have a few moments of privacy. I would seek the sun, and upon finding it I would bathe myself like a cat in a pool of warmth and savor my newly emerging independence. No one needed to know where I was during those times, and that fleeting sense of privacy—never easy to achieve inside such a large institution—gave me peace and a sense of self. It also helped prepare me for the way ahead.

Because of the attention my story had received, photographers wanted to take pictures of my departure and my return home. Fortunately, though, we were able to persuade them not to cover my departure and allow me to make the trip privately, as I wished. I had walked out of the Weill Cornell burn unit, and now, feeling glorious, I walked out of Burke. I hardly felt like Superwoman, but I did feel enormously relieved to be shedding the role of Superpatient that I'd played the last three months.

Greg helped me into the car and buckled me in, and then we rode down the long driveway without looking back. As we drove south along the Hudson River, I listened to music and gazed out the window at all that was the same and all that had changed. When my feet touched the cobblestones of Perry Street, I knew that the insulated world I'd left behind was forever gone. Our arms entwined, Greg and I walked through the door of our building.

I was greeted first by Eduardo, our doorman of many years. All smiles, he carefully hugged me and gave me a big "welcome home." After riding the elevator to the third floor, I walked down my hallway as I had so many times before. Greg opened the door to our apartment, and the moment I stepped inside my eyes were flooded with light from the early afternoon sun. Joyce, who had been the last person I'd seen when I left six months earlier, was the first person I saw as I now returned. She and I embraced as people do who have together carried the weight of something very heavy. And as we cried and held each other, we both knew that the little boy enjoying his nap down the hall had saved me, had been the true beacon guiding me home.

In the week before my return, the madcap makeover of our apartment had finally been completed. The renovation had taken eighteen months, which didn't seem possible given that we lived in only 1,300 square feet of space. But the day before my departure from Burke, Greg had assured me that the floors were refinished, the walls painted, the bathrooms done. Lights, closets, action!

Now, standing in our renovated apartment, I felt overwhelmed. The sense of dislocation hit me like a wave. I was reeling, elated to be back but also sad that so much was different. I was also struggling to accept the knowledge that from this point on there would be no cushion between reality and me. No hospital cocoon, no filtering, no cosseted understanding of what I had endured.

Caleigh helped me begin to make the transition. She had lived with our friends the Halperts, who would continue to care for her for almost a year. But Greg brought her over for a visit that afternoon, and after missing her terribly, I was thrilled to see her. Holding her, and then taking a nap with her at my side, was another way to convince myself that I was really home.

At dinner that first night, Tyler once again sat between Greg and me. Tyler and I were both learning to eat with utensils, although he was more successful than I at maintaining a grip on his spoon. I looked around the dining table, astonished to be sitting there with my husband and my son. Just the three of us having a meal—no trays, no lines, no hospital cafeteria. I was home, and we were a family again. I was *home*.

In addition to having my family around me, I was fortunate to have twenty-four-hour companion care. Though desperate for privacy and self-sufficiency, I could do almost nothing on my own. I still wore my compression garments, which meant that I couldn't go to the bathroom unassisted. I couldn't manipulate the garments' buttons and clasps, and my hands weren't strong enough to pull off the thick, elastic fabric. In fact, any activity that required dexterity presented a major challenge, and I was easily fatigued.

Every time I turned around, I encountered another task I couldn't perform. I couldn't change a diaper. I couldn't cook or prepare any but the simplest meals. The kitchen was particularly fraught with danger; given my injuries, knives, glass, and heat were a toxic mix. Even sitting still for any length of time wasn't easy: the tops of my thighs continued to bleed, and I had several open wounds and unhealed areas.

Our home was filled with flowers that arrived in a continual flow for the next several months. I thought of them as amulets of love, and they filled the house with beauty. (We collected so many vases that we eventually donated them to our local florist, who was happy to restock his shelves.) To celebrate my arrival at home, my friends at Cantor Fitzgerald sent me an enormous balloon arrangement that stood eight feet tall and five feet wide, a magnificent bouquet of Mylar and whimsy that Tyler delighted in knocking around.

And always there was Tyler. Every day we played, we hugged, and we laughed. Sometimes my laughter would be mixed with tears. "They're happy tears," I would tell Tyler. "Mommy is crying because she's happy." I couldn't stop them from coming.

The Monday after I returned home, I started what I considered my new job. Of course, this job was a lot like the old one, but instead of going down the hall for hours of therapy, now I traveled to New York-Presbyterian Hospital five days a week. (Due to my level of disability, I took a car service, and every morning we would ride downtown and loop around the Battery past Ground Zero, which was rimmed by a chain link fence and surrounded by trucks, construction crews, and ever-present visitors.) On Saturdays, Robin Silver, my extraordinarily committed OT from the Burn Center, would come to treat me at home. She had taken a strong personal interest in my recovery, and she and I had become friends.

Other than the trips to the hospital, though, I didn't go out much. I didn't go shopping; I didn't run any errands at all. I was doing much better, but I was still very cautious about interacting with the world at large. For the most part I remained sequestered at home, living in my castle by the river and rarely leaving my tower.

On March 30, two weeks after I came home, our dear friend Debra, a consummate hostess, threw a welcome back party for me at her home in Brooklyn. It was wonderful to be together with my friends, away from doctors and hospitals, and between happy tears I spent a lot of time smiling.

As I grew more comfortable and acclimated, I began to make occasional forays out of our apartment. Even a short trip required a great deal of calculated effort. I would begin to prepare mentally the day before, accumulating all the necessary inward and outward armor to face what awaited me beyond my door. *I'm going to do this,* I'd say to myself. *I'm going to get this done.* Each time, I had to make a conscious decision to hold my head high and get outdoors.

Most of my first excursions were brief walks around my West Village neighborhood at dusk. The Hudson River flowed a scant two hundred feet from our home. Running parallel to the river was a newly renovated park, and in spring and summer waves of seasonal flowers bloomed everywhere, intermixed with evergreens, deciduous trees, and wild roses. The piers that jutted into the river now featured shaded areas and benches so passersby could enjoy the water views. All in all, I could not have hoped for a better place to recover than this idyll that existed in my backyard.

I was also glad to be so near the site of the World Trade Center. Although the towers were no longer there, I had missed the beautiful view toward the tip of Manhattan, especially since it held the memories of all my friends and colleagues. While sitting beside the river, I could once again see the Colgate-Palmolive clock on the skyline of Jersey City. Remembrance was all around, and I particularly enjoyed recalling summer evenings when Greg and I used to walk the short mile home from work. The water would be a slice of gold in the late-day sun, and we were transported to a place of quiet respite after a day filled with ringing phones and endlessly blinking screens.

Now, sitting there at night accompanied by memories, I could almost feel the warm sunshine on my back. I longed for the day when I could once again go for a walk along the river in the sun, impervious to its rays. But for the moment, the delicacy of my skin made that impossible. I remained, as Greg said, "a nightwalker."

In May, my mom and dad came to New York for Mother's Day. I had been home nearly two months, but I was still adjusting to my new world. In many respects, the cadence of life at home remained unfamiliar and awkward.

To celebrate my first Mother's Day since my return, the table was set for a lovely buffet brunch. Platters filled with fruits and salads and pastries were arrayed around a centerpiece of fresh spring flowers. But as festive as the occasion seemed, I couldn't help feeling uneasy. That afternoon, we planned to take Tyler on his first trip to the Central Park Zoo, and the trip loomed in my mind like a thundercloud.

Tyler loved animals, so going to the zoo with him should have been the perfect family outing. But concern about entering a public space, particularly during daylight hours, nearly paralyzed me. My altered appearance was striking, and the thought of being observed by crowds of strangers filled me with dread. Instead of being fun, a trip to the zoo would put me in a situation I could neither control nor escape.

At first I told Greg I didn't think I could do it. Then I shook myself out of the dazed lethargy that sometimes descended when I felt overwhelmed, and I convinced myself that I was up to it. But minutes later I was swept once again into eddies of grief; there seemed to be no escape from my apprehension.

My worries finally began to recede when I focused on Tyler. How could I miss his first zoo safari? I wanted desperately to be there for my son, and I craved the experience of being a part of his life again. Resolved, I began putting on what I called my uniform. Over my pressure garments went black, loose-fitting pants that wouldn't show grease or any other stains from my healing buttocks; a lightweight cotton striped shirt; a khaki jacket; and a tan wide-brimmed canvas sun hat. I also wore sneakers—not my preferred casual look, but they were cushioned and soft.

Greg took a number of photos of me that day, and when I look at the pictures now I see a person who is very ill. My body is rigid and stiff; my face, covered in scars, is almost bright red; my jaw is clenched to keep my lips from pulling open; my eyes are hollowed. The pictures tell the story of the torture I had endured; whenever I glance at them, I can almost feel the bone-deep fatigue that shadowed me every day.

But on that May afternoon in 2002, I somehow found the strength to make the journey. We headed uptown from Perry Street and soon entered the Central Park Zoo through its broad, black iron gates. Turning right, we walked past the yelping sea lions toward the Children's Zoo. Here, Tyler would have a chance to feed and to touch some of the animals.

The day was warm and sunny, and the small petting zoo was crowded. Standing so close to so many people, I felt as if I were playing at the edge of a vortex—and I knew that if I gave in to the fear, I would fall in. I tried to breathe deeply to calm myself, to balance the sighs that involuntarily bled out of me.

Looking down, I gazed at my beautiful boy in his blue-and-white striped sweater and his khaki pants. His arms and hands outstretched and reaching for me, he smiled up at me and said, "Mom, Mom!" I leaned down and opened my arms; pressing him to my chest, I hugged him and rested my face against his. His presence calmed me, but as my hands dangled, virtually useless, I was unable to bear his weight. Afraid that he would fall, I urged Greg to take him back.

I took a breath and watched as Tyler reached out to pat a sheep on its head and feed a pig out of his hand. Watching his giddy reactions, we all laughed. When he saw the goats and heard their funny voices as they bleated for more food, Tyler pointed at them excitedly and looked at me with a huge smile on his face.

The fierce spring sun flooded the open walkways, and as we walked through the zoo I withered, more from the effort than the heat. I took advantage of shady spots where I could, but everywhere I was surrounded by a moving pool of people. Animated, milling about, talking and laughing, they made me feel claustrophobic and self-conscious. I could feel the stares. Seeing that I was distressed, my mom put her arm around me. I breathed and focused on Tyler and was able once again to lose myself in the enjoyment of the moment.

And with that I slipped forever into a new frontier. As the afternoon wore on, I learned to disregard the stares and ignore what I couldn't change. Watching Greg lift Tyler high so he could see over the crowds of people standing at the cages, I was filled with wonder. This little boy, my beloved son, had been the guidepost of my reinvention; now, seeing his hungry curiosity and innocent pleasure in such brilliant relief, I felt him beckoning and replenishing me.

To get up every day, to go outside, to be fully present in everyday life—all of this required a deep and daily commitment.

I realized that sometimes in the past I used to adjust my level of commitment to a task based on whether I thought I could actually succeed. If the likelihood of winning was small, why knock myself out? Now I had committed myself to making every possible effort to recover—to regain function in a certain joint, to break past a psychological barrier, or anything else—and go as far as those efforts took me. If my progress was slow or if I failed,

I would simply have to live with it. I promised myself that I would be strong enough to feel at peace no matter what the outcome.

There were no blue ribbons to be won as there had been in the art competitions and horse shows of my childhood, but the lesson hadn't changed: all that mattered was that I focus on doing my best. Every time I stepped up to speak in front of people, every time I walked down the street, I had to recommit to that goal, even if doing my best ended in failure. Every time people would say something complimentary, I had to force myself to believe that they were being honest. I had to put aside what I really felt: that they were just feeling sorry for me and offering encouraging words that they hoped would make me feel better. Maybe they really did feel inspired. Maybe I really did make them feel better about something in their lives. I found it very difficult to believe that, but I continually reminded myself that since my injury I had witnessed plenty of evidence that humans can be selfless and loving in their response to one another. I saw that love in all the prayers and letters and beautiful things people did for me.

Most moving to me was the commitment and courage of my husband. In the days before 9/11, we had seriously questioned our relationship, but even during the darkest days of my return to the world, he was unflinching and unfailing. He was never uncomfortable around me—on the contrary, he was *proud* of me. No matter where we were, he took me by the arm and by the hand. He didn't hesitate to caress or hug the hideous mess I often felt I'd become.

Another man might have left me, and many people would have understood that he couldn't live with someone so physically altered. We've all seen it happen: when the going really gets tough, some people check out. I had stood by Greg when he was diagnosed with his brain tumor. Now, after I'd suffered the most cat-astrophic injury imaginable, he had stood by me on the first day and on every day that followed.

Even our wedding rings had new meaning for both of us. In December of 2001, just after I arrived at Burke, Greg had pur-chased a new wedding band; he'd lost the original ring years before but had never got around to replacing it. For months I had been asking Greg to call Saint Vincent's and find out if the hospi-tal had my rings and the watch I'd been wearing on 9/11. I remem-bered how hard I'd fought when the doctors proposed to cut them off instead of pull them off. Greg kept delaying, I later discovered, because he assumed they were gone. But almost a year after my injury he triumphantly returned home holding a small plastic bag with my name on it.

Holding that bag in my hand, I marveled for a moment at how ordinary and insignificant the package appeared. I thought of the trauma of that day and the desperate effort I made to save these scraps of stone and metal. Slowly I removed my engagement ring, my wedding ring, and my watch from the bag. The watch had stopped at 8:52. The brightness of the diamonds on my engage-ment ring was still evident, but they were very dirty. Covered with a fine dusting of black soot, all of the items were dull. I held them in my hand, thinking again about the morning of September 11 and how these little objects embodied all that came before and after. They were no longer two pieces of jewelry and a watch; sus-pended in time, they were reminders of two lives forever changed.

Greg showed his commitment in myriad ways, but he demon-strated it most publicly by writing a book. In the days following 9/11, he had begun sending e-mails to our families and a number of our friends as a means of keeping them informed of my progress. Composing the e-mails was a way to express both his own pain and his admiration for the courage he believed he saw in me, even as I slept. More important, he wanted all the people who cared so deeply about me to feel connected to me, to feel as if they were in my room with me. As he wrote in an e-mail on November 19, 2001, he wanted to build a network of love for me so that when I needed it, I would feel the strength and warmth of an embrace that encircled the globe. He was certain that the support and the prayers of my family and my friends could build a bridge of hope for me to cross.

Many of the people on his list collected his e-mails and eagerly awaited the next installment. Some of them forwarded the e-mails well beyond the initial circle, and before long they were being read by people throughout the world. (Much later, I heard from a number of friends that the daily updates became the highlight of their day and served as a life raft for their hopes for themselves and for others in the darkest of times.) One of Greg's college friends was now an editor at the *New York Times*, and he forwarded the e-mails to another former classmate, who asked if he could forward Greg's e-mails to his book editor. One thing led to another, and suddenly Greg was offered a contract by a major publishing house.

All this happened while I was still in my coma. Greg waited until I was once again conscious and able to make a decision, and then asked my permission to publish the collected e-mails as a book. At first I was surprised by the idea that strangers would want to read about my injury and my recovery, yet as Greg spoke further about the extraordinary response his e-mails were receiving, I realized that my story had a life beyond my family and friends and had become important to a lot of people I had never met.

After 9/11, so many stories had been told about the horror of that day and the terrible loss of life. But here was an opportunity to tell the story about one person's struggle to survive, about a mother fighting to return to her son. Greg was determined to help people see me as more than just a statistic or a gravely injured patient. He wanted the book to be a lasting tribute to me and to our relationship, a heartfelt story about a fateful confluence of courage, hope, and love.

After hearing Greg's rationale and then sorting out my own feelings about the project, I agreed to allow the book go forward. (The title of the book was *Love, Greg & Lauren*. As an act of faith Greg had signed both our names to every one of the e-mails he had sent.) Greg and I decided to donate a portion of the proceeds to the Cantor Fitzgerald Relief Fund, and it was gratifying to be able to do something to help others in an organization so close to our hearts.

As my recovery at Weill Cornell and then Burke unfolded, Greg continued to send out e-mails reporting on my progress. On March 11, the six-month anniversary of the attacks, the book was published. I left Burke and returned home a few days later, and when the book became a bestseller I couldn't help but appreciate life's ironies. Thinking back to our fierce argument on the night of September 10, when Greg spoke passionately about his desire to become a journalist and to write books, I was reminded of how little we know about what the future holds. Greg had always been a soulful, brilliant creator wrapped in a suit, and now here he was fulfilling his dream and becoming the author of a book.

As pleasing it was to see Greg's e-mails serve as the basis of a successful book, I was deeply affected by a letter Greg wrote to me soon after the book appeared. One morning, Greg handed me a folded piece of paper. Opening it, I found the following letter.

Dear Lauren,

I wrote a book about you, but I never wrote to you.

I've spoken to you a thousand times since you were able to hear me, but I've given you nothing, really, to remember me by, to hold and to look at while I'm not there, other than a wallet and some photographs. The book jacket you have was written by others.

So let me say to you, that I love you. I love you in a way that makes me cry. My entire life is about protecting you, seeing you happy again, and strong.

I see you on that path, taking firm steps every day; you have the perfect disposition to push yourself, to strive to improve your capabilities every waking moment. You're a true self starter, someone who has always decided what she wanted and gone for it with absolute commitment. That has never been—could never be— more clear than in this struggle that you are quite clearly winning.

Not just winning; going to win.

I cannot possibly imagine how difficult it is; I may think I can, but there's a difference between seeing it from your perspective, and there is never a moment that I'm not aware of that.

But there is something you should know; when you falter, and you may, I will be there to pick you back up, to lift you and carry you on. I will never leave your side. I will be there in the light, and in the darkness; I will be there in body and in spirit, because even when I'm not there, know that I believe in you.

Whenever you doubt anything, or fear anything, know that I believe; know that I will support you, know that I will assist you in any and every way that I can. If I do have power, that power is yours; if I do have strength, that strength is yours.

And know that I love our son. I see you in him; when I hold him, I hear you singing to him. There is never a moment when I think anything other than that he is your son, the one you brought into this world, the one whose face you saw in the depths of your soul as you fought to live, first running, and then lying still, but never wavering in your desire to see him again. I will take care of him too; I will protect both of you, and the only thing that you ever need to do, to satisfy me, is to hold him in your arms and smile at him.

Take your time with everything; do it right, and do it thoughtfully. Tyler and I will always be here, waiting for you; and when you are strong enough, we will always be with you.

We have all the time in the world, now, to love each other; so relax, and rest, and dream sweet dreams of our future.

Love,
Greg

With the book's publication, my story received even more attention. Another article about my recovery ran on the front page of the *New York Times.* Accompanying the piece was a picture of Greg and me; in it, he is holding me tenderly as I rest against his shoulder. We appeared on the *Oprah Winfrey Show* for a full hour; taped while I was still at Burke and so unable to travel, it featured Oprah's first-ever remote interview. I wasn't at all sure what I should wear for the appearance, and in the end I chose a red St. John suit—not the best color choice given the extreme redness and inflammation of my skin. Before the taping, a makeup artist tried to do the best she could with my wreck of a face. Especially since it was the first time I'd worn any makeup since the morning of 9/11, the experience was more than a little uncomfortable.

When it aired, the show attracted a huge audience. The deep

psychic wounds inflicted by 9/11 were still raw. Oprah gave a face and voice to those survivors who shared the experience of that painful day and told of the challenges we confronted. One legacy of the Oprah appearance was that it inspired legions of people to care about the injured of 9/11. The amazing outpouring of messages and words of encouragement that came from around the world encouraged me to believe that millions stood by me.

Greg and I were also interviewed several times by Katie Couric on the *Today Show*. In Katie, I saw something of myself: she too was a successful professional woman who had suffered a grievous loss. (Her husband died of colon cancer in 1998.) We were two hometown girls who were now living and working and raising our families in New York City. Katie had fought back after experiencing her own tragedy, and I told her I would do the same. I assured her that I would unquestionably return to full functionality, that I would regain 100 percent of what I had lost. I said it through tears, but I said it with conviction. That was my game-day mentality talking: until you're beaten, you still own the win. But this was how I chose to deal with a tough situation. Assuring people that I would achieve the perfect ending helped me avoid thinking too hard about the likely ending.

Afterward I couldn't bear to watch any of the interviews. I tried once, but the reality of what I saw was too discouraging. Looking at that poor, horribly injured woman on television, seeing all that "she" was going through, brought tears to my eyes. Instinctively I knew that it was still necessary for me to protect myself and operate on a different plane. It may have been a kind of denial, but I needed to live outside of my tattered body while I nursed it back to health.

The morning after the second *Today Show* segment aired, Greg told me that Katie Couric pronounced me her hero, one of the most remarkable women she had ever met. This gave me pause. I was uncomfortable with the notion that I was some sort of hero. To my mind, a hero is someone who has saved or defended someone else, at great personal risk and for no personal benefit. My effort may have been heroic, but on 9/11 others proved to be the real heroes.

I think of the Samaritan who came to my aid. This man, a bond salesman and the father of two children, chose to respond to the unfolding disaster not by fleeing but by helping me. Like many other civilians that day, he thought first of others instead of himself. He made a remarkable choice: he ran toward trouble instead of away from it. He has never wanted to be named, but his name is always in my prayers, and it will always be in my heart. To me, he is a true hero.

I feel the same way about Brian Clark, who was one of the two best men at our wedding. Brian was standing on the eighty-fourth floor of the South Tower when the opposite corner of that floor was struck by the second plane. The building twisted and swayed from the torque of the impact. Brian and his six coworkers froze in shock; moments later, they started down the stairs. When they encountered a woman and a man coming up the stairs and warning of fire on the floors below, the rest of Brian's group turned back. But Brian had heard a man calling for help; after locating the source of the voice in the rubble, he reached through destroyed framing and Sheetrock and, with a strength that can't be explained, pulled the man to safety. (Astonishingly, this man had looked into the eyes of the hijackers as they flew the plane into the tower.) Brian and his charge then continued down the stairs, at last reaching the ground floor and dodging debris as they crossed Liberty Street. They escaped the building with barely a scratch and had walked only five blocks when the building collapsed behind them. From the group of six coworkers who had turned back upstairs, only one other person survived.

So if I wasn't a hero, what was I? I was a survivor. I had suffered life-threatening injuries and now carried disfiguring scars, so perhaps it was a courageous thing to stand up and say, "I'm still here." Sometimes, my instincts had told me to run, to hide myself. Perhaps to do the opposite—to face new people and new situations and say, in effect, "I am not asking for your respect; I'm demanding it by my presence and my actions"—has been one of the bravest things I've ever done. And yes, many people did tell me that I led them by example, that my actions had raised the standard of what they demanded from themselves. By saying this they honored me not as someone whom they pitied, but as someone who helped show them how to conquer their own adversity.

Even so, I couldn't rescue anybody on that September morning. I couldn't change what happened to so many people I knew. The only thing I could do was to fight back by living. Reflecting on what I had done since being injured, I decided that I wasn't a hero and didn't need to be one. I simply had to find the courage to honor my obligations to my family and the strength to fulfill my duty to all those who would never have the opportunity to fight for themselves.

That spring and early summer, I would often lie awake at night listening to the caravans of trucks rumbling up the West Side Highway. Many of them were hauling away the ruins of the World Trade Center. To me, every roar of their engines' gears reverberated with the knowledge of a world still filled with pain and sorrow.

In August, we spent a week in Pine Plains at our house on Carpenter Hill Road. A Cape Cod center-hall farmhouse set into the hillside, it was successor to a mobile home that had formerly stood in the shadow of the neighborhood gravel mine, though the crown of the mine—which had once been behind the property to the south—was long gone. We looked north out onto rolling hills, giant green waves seemingly frozen in a single instant. A couple of years earlier we had begun to reclaim six acres from the former mine, grading the weathered skin of loosely crumbled stone. Now the rocky field was slowly becoming a gentle meadow of tall grasses that changed colors as they bent to the passing breeze.

The air that week was hot and still, as it often is in the summer in that part of the Hudson Valley. I felt claustrophobic in the heat, encased as I was in my ever-present pressure garments. But I relished watching Tyler splash about in his backyard wading pool, smiling and laughing with Caleigh at his side. I would don my hat and protective sun gear, and we would take short walks in the meadow and along the roads past the horse farms. It was profoundly satisfying to be communing with my son and watching him savor his early encounters with nature. I called us the Carpenter Hill Explorers Club.

"Mom, look!" he would say, lifting up a small stone flecked with glittering mica.

"Wow, Tyler," I'd reply. "That can be your special treasure."

After this brief escape, a new challenge loomed: the first anniversary of 9/11. I dreaded the day, and for the entire week leading up to it desperate memories filled every corner of my mind.

The anniversary provided an opportunity for the entire nation to examine both what was lost on 9/11 and what was gained in its aftermath. For me, conversations about the day and its powerful reverberations were often very difficult, because they forced me to relive the horror and heartache of the attacks. But I also discovered that whenever I spoke to people about what had happened to me, they invariably began to relate their own experiences of 9/11. They would tell me about being at the World Trade Center, or somewhere else in Manhattan, or watching television on the other side of the country or the world. They would tell me about people they knew who had died, or about spouses who served in the armed forces and had been deployed to Afghanistan in the weeks and months after the war began. By acknowledging their pain and trying to ease their grief, or by thanking them for their service to our country, I was able to help others to heal. As well, I was doing what I could to help preserve the unity and understanding that had filled the hearts of so many in the wake of the attacks.

I was honored to be recognized by several organizations around the time of the anniversary. *Glamour* magazine named me one of its Women of the Year, and the award was presented to me by Senator Clinton, who had received the same honor the previous year. The post-award reception was held in the Temple of Dendur at the Metropolitan Museum of Art. Bernie Cantor had been a patron of the museum, and several times the Met had served as the site of Cantor Fitzgerald's annual client party. As I looked around the cavernous open space laced with reflecting pools, I could almost hear the talk and laughter of clients, colleagues, and friends from those long-ago evenings. Those wonderful times were sealed in a past as distant as the ancient collection housed in the room.

Greg and I also were among four honorees at "Without Fear," an event sponsored by the Anti-Defamation League at the John F.

Kennedy Center for the Performing Arts. But the occasion that meant the most to me occurred on the anniversary of 9/11 itself, when at Howard's invitation Greg and I spoke at Cantor Fitzgerald's memorial service.

The sky on September 11, 2002, was jewel-blue, just as it had been the previous year. The city sparkled in the clear sun, and the driving winds made the day at once beautiful and tumultuous. The service was due to be held at the SummerStage in Central Park, just inside the entrance to the park at Seventy-second Street and Fifth Avenue. The company's first memorial service, just three weeks after 9/11, had been held there too. Remembering those weeks when I had lain in a hospital bed while my mind journeyed through a world of cages and cliff people, I found it hard to believe that a full year had passed. And today, instead of a head-to-toe sari of bandages, I wore a black Armani suit and heels. It was only the second time I'd worn heels since 9/11, but since they didn't require me to bend my ankles too much, they suited my peg legs just fine.

The memorial was scheduled to begin at 4:00 p.m. Not wanting to be late, we made sure to leave by 3:15. Our plan was to take a taxi north along the West Side Highway and Tenth Avenue, and then cut across the park at Sixty-sixth Street. But when we reached the West Sixties, we discovered that all the streets around Columbus Circle had been closed. The day's high winds had blown construction materials off the partially completed AOL Time Warner Tower; one person had been killed, another had been critically injured, and a number of windows had been smashed, so the area had been cordoned off.

Traffic came to a dead stop. Five and then ten minutes passed, and still we were barely moving. Frantic, Greg got out of the car and pleaded with police officers at one barricade after another to let us through. When that failed, he explained that I was due to speak at an important memorial service and asked for some assistance to get us across the park. A police sergeant pointed down the block toward his supervisor, but when Greg jogged over, the supervisor refused even to acknowledge his presence. To him, Greg was just a distraction, an intense guy in a suit running along the yellow caution tape and begging for help.

With time running out, we decided to get out of the cab and walk. Given my still-shaky limbs, I wouldn't be able to maneuver well in high heels, but this was our only option. We started east across Sixty-sixth Street, crossing Columbus Avenue and then Broadway at a near jog. After just a single block I was aching, sweating, and out of breath. Moving as fast as we could, we continued to the far side of the restricted zone at Central Park West, where, much to our relief, Greg spotted an empty cab. We jumped in and arrived at the service several minutes later. The program was already well under way, but we took our seats and felt lucky to have made it.

Both of New York's then-senators spoke at the service that afternoon. Senator Charles Schumer called the high winds that swept Manhattan on this first anniversary of the attacks the tumult of restless souls. Senator Clinton spoke movingly about Cantor Fitzgerald's losses and hailed the way that the firm had coped and rebuilt; she also mentioned having met me during my rehabilitation at Burke and offered some very generous words about how much she admired my strength.

Shortly before it was our turn to speak, Greg and I were taken up to the dais. Sitting next to Howard and looking straight into the blazing sun, I could see little in front of me. As Greg and I waited for the other speakers to finish, Howard shielded my eyes, and I saw that thousands of people had gathered to pay tribute to all those who had died. Mothers, fathers, wives, children, sisters, and brothers—here in front of me was the living connection to my lost friends. After all the hope they'd given me, all their prayers, I felt an enormous sense of loyalty and indebtedness. I wanted to embrace them all, to hold them and somehow take their pain away. Once again I felt deep anger at what had happened, but I also felt grateful for the opportunity to at last pay tribute before so many of those who had shared such an extraordinary loss.

Greg spoke first, and after he finished he stood beside me. In my remarks, I mourned the passing of so many, but I also said that I wished for joy and for a celebration of full and happy lives.

To paraphrase a line from Dylan Thomas, "I would like to rage against the dying of their light." I want to cry out loud to remember my friends. Instead of standing for a moment of silent prayer, I want to clap until my arms ache, to make so much noise so that God can hear us, so that everyone can hear us, and most of all so that they can hear us. I want them to know that we celebrate the time we had with them, and that we will never, never surrender our memories of them.

Their lives were not about sadness and loss; their lives were filled with energy, love, faith, and, most of all, hope for the future. I wish—I hope—they can hear us say, *You lived well, and we will always love you.*

The service was graced by some beautiful music, with songs performed by both Judy Collins and the Harlem Boys Choir. But the most moving moments came at the end when the names of the Cantor Fitzgerald employees who had perished were read aloud. One by one, 658 names rang out, testimony to the people we had lost in that insane and terrible atrocity.

During my speech, when I said that I would wish for joy and spoke of my desire to clap so loudly that the lost might hear us, a chorus of cheers rose up from the crowd. For a fleeting moment, the love for so many who had died was able to take a form other than tears. When I finished, the audience rose to its feet, celebrating all those we held so close to our hearts.

8

ENDURANCE

Sure I am of this, that you have only to endure to conquer. You
have only to persevere to save yourselves.

—WINSTON CHURCHILL

During the languid summers of my childhood, when we kids
were on vacation from school, we were always looking for things
to do. One lazy afternoon when I was eleven, my sister, Gigi, and my
brother, Scot, took up a game of tennis behind the house. They got
into an argument almost immediately, and soon they were running
after each other, their tennis racquets now makeshift weapons. My
brother fled through the backyard around the side of the house
only to be met by my fleet-footed sister. Turning, he ran through
the garage and out the back door, slamming it shut just as my sister's hand raised to stop it. Her hand smashed through the door's
window, and the shattered pane sliced into her wrist.

As Gigi tried to cover the deep cut, blood spouted to the ceiling. Scot ran to get my mother. I was upstairs in my room reading;
though I'd heard my sister and brother screaming, I really became
alarmed when my mother yelled for me. I ran downstairs, opened

the door to the garage, and was immediately hit by the smell of fresh blood. A large part of the garage floor had been shellacked red, and the ceiling was spattered with red as if someone had decorated it with spin art.

My mother shouted at me to get a towel while she grabbed the car keys. As soon as I found a towel, I wrapped it around Gigi's wrist; by then, she was in agony and in shock. But the blood continued to pour out, and when the towel was saturated in less than a minute, I yelled for Scot to get me another one. I wrapped the second towel as tightly as I could around my sister's slight wrist and held it, squeezing with all my strength.

We threw ourselves in the car and sped through the streets, the horn blaring. Tears streamed down Gigi's face; her eyes wide, she pleaded with me to not squeeze so hard. I ignored her. By now the towel had soaked red again, but I continued to squeeze it as hard as I could, willing my sister to live. "Stop!" Gigi yelled. "You are holding too tight! I can't feel my hand!" But she could shout at me all she liked: I wasn't going to let go. And all the way to the hospital I was absolutely clear about what I needed to do. I didn't care what it took, I would stop the blood.

A quart of blood and a long string of stitches later, Gigi came home. She had lost mobility and strength in her hand, and it would never fully return. But that was all she lost. Nothing else mattered, because I still had my sister.

This was the moment when I learned that I could stay calm in a crisis. Just as important, I proved to myself that I could hold on for dear life as long as I needed to. That belief in my own toughness never left me; years later, both during and after 9/11, it proved crucial to my own survival.

By the beginning of 2003, I was no longer carried forward by the euphoria I'd felt when I realized that I would survive my injuries. Instead, I relied on my emotional stamina to stay the course. I had gotten through the most critical part of my recovery, but a hard road still stretched in front of me, with no end in sight. That winter and spring, I had surgeries about every eight weeks; over the summer, I took a break so that I could heal. As far as I had come, I knew I had completed only the first leg of an epic physical and emotional marathon.

Most of the surgeries were on my hands. They always seemed to be in a cast, and for months I was either healing from the last surgery or preparing for the next, steeling myself like a boxer preparing for a new opponent. I also underwent significant surgeries to release the scar tissue that was binding my torso and the left side of my neck. In one operation, I had a large amount of scar tissue cut away, after which an experimental material called Integra was used to graft a portion of my left flank from my underarm to my waist. This material had to be irrigated every four hours for weeks, so my body was always wet, but the result would be more pliable skin.

The treatment to release a scar on the left side of my neck was equally unpleasant. Dr. Lloyd Gayle inserted a balloon under the skin at the base of the left side of my neck, and every week over the course of several months they slowly inflated it with water so that the skin would adapt and stretch. The result was that in addition to my facial scars, I had an ever-expanding goiter on the side of my neck that grew increasingly difficult to disguise. My Hermès scarves saw a lot of action that year.

Despite all the progress I'd made, I was still caught in the eye of the storm that had become my life. A typical day would include a trip to Dr. Yurt; he would examine the Integra graft on my flank and say it looked good, and then we'd have more discussions of how much longer I'd be wearing my pressure garments. (Another summer to go in the zoot suit, longer still for my hands.) He would look at the patches of red and pink skin covering my body, all of it indicating both bad news (continued inflammation) and good news (I was still healing). We would discuss the list of operations still to come, among them redoing the graft on my left hand with Integra and removing hypertrophic scarring on my upper back. He would then examine my face. "Oh yes," he'd say, "the skin is soft and improving." Words, words, and more words— a pounding torrent of information about what was still to come. More operations, more hospital stays, more scar management, more pain.

After Dr. Yurt I would visit Dr. Olivier Nicolay, my orthodontist. It felt more than a little odd to be seeing an orthodontist at the age of forty-two. But because I'd continually bitten down on the breathing tube during the first four weeks of my intubation, I had done some real damage to my teeth. My top front teeth had been pushed apart, my top and bottom front teeth crossed each other, and two of my teeth had cracked. The cracks could wait, because first I had to get braces. Braces—no question that this would be a real good look. Then again, given the way my face looked, I figured no one would notice.

Valentine's Day 2003 fell on a Friday, and that evening Greg took me to dinner at the Stissing House, the restored inn at the center of Pine Plains. The second floor of the inn was a performance space, and soon after we entered the restaurant and sat down we heard some familiar music. Madeleine Peyroux, we discovered, was playing a show directly upstairs. Although there were no tickets available, we could hear the music well enough to enjoy it.

When the band ended its first set, Greg stepped away for a few minutes. Shortly after he returned, Madeleine Peyroux herself walked up to us carrying her guitar and accompanied by her bass and harmonica players. Smiling, she introduced each of her band members and then proceeded to perform "Walkin' After Midnight" right beside our table. Listening to the song and remembering how I had danced with nine-month-old Tyler, the spirit of that beautiful summer of 2001 came achingly alive.

I was glad to have such a moment of joy, because that spring, as I started into a new round of surgeries, I hit a low point. I had so many more operations ahead of me, and my life seemed to revolve around their scheduling. More than a year and a half after my injury, I expected a payoff for all my hard work, but there didn't seem to be one. The surgeries were a series of waves that washed continually over me. Just as I'd get my head above water and gasp for air, I would go under again. I told Greg that all the operations felt like "a controlled assault on my body." I gave up even counting them.

From time to time, Senator Clinton would check in with me and ask how I was doing. During one phone conversation I told her, "I'm slowly digging myself out of the hole. But I always have the feeling and knowledge that I'll be pummeled again. The upside, I suppose, is that I know it's happening, which makes it somewhat easier to handle."

I wished I knew when the surgeries would end. At Burke, I'd spent weeks longing to know when I would be released; when Dr. Novitch had finally given me a date, I'd felt tremendously liberated. Now I had no such completion date to look forward to, making my recovery much more difficult to manage psychologically. With so many hurdles obstructing a clear view of the future, I did my best to live in the present. But more often than I care to remember, I found myself contemplating a past that no longer was and a future that never could be.

Most difficult of all, though, was that I often had to keep my distance from Tyler. If he knocked me the wrong way, he might tear a patch of skin off my body or pop the neck balloon. My flesh was still very raw, and the potential for disastrous infection was always very real. But since I didn't want him to worry about me or feel abandoned, I continued to spend as much time with him as possible.

Whenever we were together, I would protect my face and be especially careful with my hands. He would look at the ever-growing lump on my neck with concern and ask me to lay my head back on the couch as I read to him. Wanting desperately to be close to him, I would lie prone next to him as we read books together. Even though I knew that his perpetually moving arms could cause major damage, I trusted that he would be careful.

Later that spring Dr. Gayle finally removed the neck balloon. I'll never forget asking my aide at the time, "Does it look better? Does it look better?" I was so eager to hear that my neck looked better, but she replied, "No, not really." She was undoubtedly right: after a surgery like that one there was always inflammation and swelling, so if anything my neck probably looked worse. Even so, I found her answer terribly discouraging; it was one more reminder of how far I had to go.

In June I tried kicking around a red ball with Tyler in the hallway outside our apartment. My left foot bumped the wall after a casual kick, and I felt a sharp pain. The X-rays showed a hairline fracture on the outside of my foot. But they also revealed a poorly healed broken ankle, and I recalled the crack I'd felt as I'd run from the World Trade Center. The break had been so far down on the list of my injuries after 9/11 that no one had paid any attention to it, and the ankle had healed on its own. This explained why my ankle had continued to give me such trouble, so now, after the hairline fracture healed, my physical therapy focused on rebuilding my ankle strength.

I still found every day a major physical challenge. The simple act of raising my arm or walking required a focused effort. Because the wounds on my buttocks had still not healed, I had to use an air cushion whenever I sat down. Every evening Kareen's long elegant fingers would gently move over my taut skin, trying to extract some suppleness from my harsh red grafts. It was often excruciating, and our nightly routine lasted three hours. When I ate, I used a modified spoon and fork, but even then the effort to hold and direct the utensils would leave me tired at the end of every meal, my hand painful and weak. Meanwhile, my healing body remained in an incredible state of overdrive. My heart rate was still in the 100s, and three times a day I was still consuming a protein drink containing a thousand calories—and that was before I ate anything else.

I also found myself increasingly haunted by the possibility that terrorists would once again strike New York City. By the fall of 2003, the United States was at war in both Iraq and Afghanistan, and the government's security offensive was in full swing. A color-coded alert system was getting a lot of attention, and regular reports of terrorist activity—especially one about a plan to blow up the Brooklyn Bridge—put me on edge. With soldiers manning all the major routes into and out of the city, everyone seemed consumed by the thought that terrorists would return and launch a new attack.

A cottage industry dedicated to personal security sprang up, and numerous firms began selling everything from survival kits to gas masks. At one point there was actually a shortage of masks, so I felt lucky when, after days of research and agonizing, I was able to buy four of the type I had chosen. One of the masks was for Greg; he had started taking the subway to work, and New York's elaborate public transportation system was an obvious potential target. I gave two masks to Joyce and asked her to keep them near her at all times so she could protect Tyler and herself, since to my mind some coward was as likely to blow himself up at the playground as at any other place. The last mask I kept for myself, hoping I'd have time to tape plastic on our windows and wind up the portable radio before keeling over if and when the terrorists struck.

It's all quite fantastic in retrospect, little better than a child's strategy for warding off the terror demons. But the ever-present threat of terrorism had wrapped its tentacles around me and seemed to be squeezing me more tightly with each passing week. Every day I prayed that nothing would happen to Greg and Tyler. At night, I would fervently bargain with God, asking God to take me in the event of another attack, and spare them. Worrying about the possibility that the terrorists would come back and hurt my family drove me to the edge of exhaustion, and often I couldn't sleep without taking medication.

I had always believed myself to be a strong person, but sometimes I would stand in the shower as the warm water poured over my body, searching for solace. I still had so much left to do, and so much time was being stolen from me. I would gaze at my hands and feel despair over the prospect of yet another surgery on them. Waves of sadness would wash over me, and I would cover my face with my hands and cry. But then, slowly, I would pull myself together and once again remind myself of the obvious. *I am glad to have my hands at all. And it could have been worse—I am incredibly lucky to be alive.*

Then there were the ordinary terrors that happen in every life, such as those that occur when loved ones die too soon. On September 29, we learned that our dear friend Bill Bennett, one of the founding members of Greg's band, had been in a serious car accident. While driving his beat-up old van in Manhattan, he was hit while traveling at a low speed by a vehicle that had run a red light. Bill wasn't wearing a seat belt, and when the impact opened the van's door he tumbled out and slammed his head on the pavement. Though he said he felt okay, he was taken to Bellevue Hospital, where he learned he had a severe concussion.

Bill's passion in life was music. An accomplished guitarist and bass player, he and his band opened for the Ramones a few times. He and Greg first met in the summer of 1993 in a rehearsal studio on Murray Street. Bill was putting a band together—the band that became the Rolling Bones—and he asked Greg to be the bass player. I had met Bill in 1997, and the three of us had been close ever since.

Soon after the accident, Bill took a turn for the worse. At first the hospital had restricted visitors to Bill's immediate family, but now we were told that friends would be permitted to visit as well. On October 4, Greg and I arrived at Bellevue at about 7:00 p.m. and went to the fourth-floor ICU. It was extremely quiet. When a nurse took us to Bill's bedside, we found him lying in the troubled peace that surrounds those who have been seriously injured and then sedated. The day before, he had developed a highly resistant MRSA infection and entered a coma. I knew all about the dangers of lethal infections, and now Bill's body was being flooded with powerful antibiotics in a desperate effort to save him.

Greg and I leaned in close. The nurses told us that even in a coma you can still hear things; I knew that to be true, so we spoke to Bill with encouraging words. I said. "Come on, Billy, we need you. You can do it. Everything's going to be all right." Platitudes, indeed, but they are about the best anyone can do when standing at the bedside of someone who is seriously injured or very ill. We stayed until the end of visiting hours, and I prayed hard that night through clenched fists, sure my prayers would work.

But on October 7, Greg got a call telling him that Bill had died. We were devastated—Bill had touched the lives of so many over the years. A week later, the *New York Times* ran an obituary alongside a picture of Bill wearing his typical look of bemused seriousness. Seeing his name in print helped give us some sense of resolution and confirmed that he would never be forgotten.

Later, at a memorial service to celebrate Bill's life, the rooms overflowed with people. But I was jarred once again by this reminder of how unyielding death is, and how rarely it gives a reprieve. How could he have left us in an instant? It was unthinkable, and I felt the return of a dull ache deep in my gut, just like the one that had gripped me when I finally learned about all my friends who had died on 9/11.

Sometimes that fall I was tempted to capitulate to fear and despair, but anger and determination always pulled me back from the edge. I would wake up thinking, *You are here, this is now, there is no time to waste.* I would lie in bed contemplating the importance of the human beings who surrounded me and remember that the impact we can have on one another's lives is immense. *Take the joy and goodness while you can,* I would tell myself, *because it's not going to last all that long. We always think it will, and it never does.*

One of the ways I fed my determination to move forward was

by sorting through my closet full of clothes. Some of my dresses had been resurrected; many I would never wear again. There they hung, ladies in waiting, vestiges of a life long gone. But I couldn't give them away or throw them out; angry, I would tell myself that the terrorists may have tried to steal my very life, but they weren't getting my beautiful summer dresses. At first I would try on a dress, look in the mirror, and say to myself, *No, absolutely no way.* Then I would convince myself that I could wear it only in the dark. But finally I began to say, *Oh come on, why not? Sure, you can see the scars, but since when is everyone else so perfect?*

I was graced with absolute acceptance and love from Greg, who would often say (then and now), "Lauren, you are a beautiful woman; you can wear anything you want." His words defined love, and I would play them over and over in my head, their echo and resonance feeding me. But even though Greg had anointed me the Princess of Perry Street, my return felt nothing like a fairy tale with a happy ending. Everything was eerily the same, but I was radically different, and sometimes I felt that I was a reminder of times that people would rather forget. Feelings of ugliness and imperfection gripped me. In a world preoccupied with physical beauty, I struggled with a low self-image. But how could I ask my son, or my husband, or the world to accept me if I couldn't find a way to accept myself?

In truth, even though my body was still hobbled and weak, I was already holding myself accountable to fashion once again. Every time I thought about going to the store, or taking my son on a play date, or going out with friends, I would pause for a moment of self-evaluation and think about what would be appropriate and what wouldn't. Whatever I chose to wear, I was sure that there would be some furtive stares and scrutiny. In a few cases, I had to accept the fact that a place or a situation would make me feel physically uncomfortable, and so I would decide not to go.

I had been knocked badly out of balance, but I recognized that for this fairy tale to end happily, the princess needed to slay the dragon. So one night I drew myself up and decided to do just that. With a nod to vanity, I powdered my nose and put on a rich coral-and-peach lipstick. I applied mascara to my light eyelashes and slipped on the perfect little black dress and a pair of four-inch Christian Louboutin heels. I made a conscious decision to face the stares and hear the whispering when I went out. And there were stares, but I realized rather quickly that I simply didn't care.

It took time, but finally I began to feel comfortable with my body again. I released myself from the pressures of beauty's "shoulds." I reminded myself once more that I was fortunate to be alive to worry about beauty at all; besides, the mere fact that I could put most clothes on myself was a major accomplishment. Ignoring the mass of crosshatched scars that laced my skin, I dreamed I was perfect. *This is who I am,* I told myself, *and if they have a problem, they can look the other way.*

My mother's hands were always manicured, painted with the perfect red shade, and my father's hands were similarly neat and tended. But the earliest memory I have of my hands is looking down at the short, torn edges of my nails and the raw red skin around them. When I was young, I used to pick at them constantly, and my mother and father would often chastise me and insist that I stop. When that didn't work, my mother threatened to put some foul-tasting potion on my fingers. Once I became a fashion-conscious teenager, I finally stopped picking at them, and from then on proudly tended to my long and newly graceful nails.

Now my nails and hands were anything but beautiful, and one day I found myself looking down at them, thinking about their history. My hands were leathered, resembling deformed claws, and the nails that topped the wrinkled bony appendages were twisted and very thick. The damage done to the nail beds of my right hand had caused the broken, calcified nails to take on the jagged appearance of an eagle's talon. My left hand was much worse: a few of the fingertips had been amputated, and those that remained were malformed and carried slivers that barely resembled nails.

But as bad as my hands looked, I decided that it was time to do something about them. I asked Kareen to try clipping my nails, and as the nail clipper removed thick chunks of keratin with a loud crack, I cringed and wanted to pull away. When she finished, we looked down and agreed that my hands looked marginally better—at least I could no longer use them as a defensive weapon. Having come this far, I asked Kareen if she would file the tops and try to make them thinner. It hurt, but she did it, and once again they looked slightly better.

Encouraged by Kareen's handiwork, I worked up the nerve to ask Olga Vidov, the owner of Gemini, a local salon, if someone in her shop would understand my situation and be willing to give me a manicure. A few days later, I crossed over to the shaded side of Perry Street to avoid the sun and walked the three blocks to Olga's salon with my daytime aide, Lesma Williams, beside me. When we arrived, I turned to Lesma and told her I could do this myself. Once inside, I was escorted to a treatment room and introduced to a manicurist named Vicky.

Vicky was a petite, blond Russian woman with a strong accent and a personality to match. She took my hand, looked nonplussed, and said, "Yes, yes, of course we can fix, we can make better. They will look beautiful—beautiful." As only a Russian speaking accented English can, she pronounced it *buut-e-ful*. I nodded my head, skeptical but encouraged, and sat down, peering nervously to the left and right in the hope that no one would take the seats on either side of her station. I had another reason to be anxious: Dr. Weiland had warned me that if I got a manicure I risked infection and injury, which could easily cost me part of a finger.

Vicky confidently took my mangled, tremulous right hand and started filing. She didn't cringe, and she didn't treat me with kid gloves. The pressure on my fingers and skin was extremely painful. But Vicky kept chatting, distracting me while she carefully glued a silk wrap on my hand's split index nail, binding the two halves together. Then she built up the runt of the pinky nail and filed down the rest of the clawlike nails. I decided that the less my hands were noticed the better, and that the best way to counterbalance the yellowed color of my nails was with a French manicure, which, with its flesh tones and white tips, is designed to resemble natural nails. No more of the reds or deep colors that I had taken to wearing right before 9/11.

As Vicky cleaned and pushed back the two remaining cuticles on my right hand, I looked on, amazed at the transformation taking place. Suddenly it looked more like a hand and not quite as deformed. Once Vicky applied the topcoat to the nails, I bent my hand up slightly and gazed at the astonishing piece of art she had created. Tears welled up in my eyes and my voice broke as I reached over to embrace and thank her.

A small part of the woman I had once been had returned. Although different, my hand once again looked beautiful to me.

That fall, I finally felt ready to go out to the movies again. Lesma helped me prepare for this outing by putting a pair of lightweight wool pants over my pressure garments. She unclipped the clear plastic mask from my face, removed it, and wiped it off with alcohol both to keep it clean and to protect the integrity of the silicone lining. The mask now sat on the vanity counter and stared back at me with its two gaping eyeholes. Void of color, it looked haunted. It reminded me of Edvard Munch's *The Scream,* the painting in which an agonized figure stands on a bridge set against a flaming sunset, his mouth gaping in a silent scream—and the image that still evokes all the terror and pain of 9/11 more than any other. I threw a towel over it.

Ideally the mask came off just twice a day, and even then only for the length of time it took me to shower. I was meticulous about following this mandate; I slept with it on, and only on the rare occasions when I went out socially did I remove it. With just three small openings that permitted me to see clearly and to breathe, the mask fit so tightly to the contours of my face that it was a virtual part of me, transforming me, pressing the hardened skin beneath so the inflammations morphed like the liquid in a lava lamp. The scars, I had learned, had a life of their own, some spreading and rising, others collapsing. The changes required that my face be periodically remeasured for a new mask, as if the spirits in the mask were continually re-forming and reshaping my identity.

Now, without my mask on, I looked at myself in the mirror and saw the late afternoon light striking the right side of my face. The eddies of scar tissue that might be hidden by a softer light were laid bare, and I realized that my face bore the treacherous map of the journey I had taken. Turning to Lesma, I asked her to pull off my right-hand glove. Somewhat clumsily, I used my hand to apply makeup in an effort to cover the scars. After Greg helped me on with my jacket, I carefully put my ungloved hand into one of the pockets, neatly out of sight. Finally we were ready to go.

We walked a few blocks over to a nearby movie theater. It was early evening, and the theater was nearly empty. Once one of the grand old movie palaces, it was a bit shabby by then; the foyer under the fluorescent lights smelled slightly musty, and a lone concession stand dispensed soda, bottles of water, and what appeared to be premade popcorn.

We had our choice of seats and soon settled in to watch *Something's Gotta Give*, a romantic comedy starring Diane Keaton and Jack Nicholson. The film was light and funny, and both of us laughed often. At one point Greg looked over at me and said, "I love hearing you laugh." I smiled, and a moment later he slipped his hand through my right hand, slowly wrapping his fingers through my fingers, pressing his palm against mine. For the first time since my injury, he was holding my hand without a glove. I welcomed the tingling pleasure of his skin against mine; it felt so normal. But it also felt strangely new, because unlike that long-ago movie night during my time at Burke, no pain accompanied the pressure of his hand holding mine. I felt like a teenager on a date feeling a boy's romantic touch for the first time, and I was returned to that happiness I'd known so rarely the previous two years.

My family was my reason for living, and as I became stronger and better able to venture out in the world, I decided to make the most of our time together. Thursdays became Tyler Day, and each week we'd choose a destination for a search-and-explore mission. I remember especially enjoying our visit to the American Museum of Natural History. As our taxi wound toward the Central Park West entrance, Tyler pointed out trucks and buses to our right and left while clutching his tiger, the animal of the day. Usually he was holding a lion; in fact, usually he thought he *was* a lion. In moments of uncertainty or frustration, he would rear back his head and let loose a roar that was so realistic he'd startle passersby. I understood this as his defense mechanism, a show of strength against all the frightening things that had become part of his daily life.

"Mommy, we going to go see the animals!" he exclaimed excitedly. "That's right," I said, "we're going to the museum." I broke into song: "*We're gonna have a good time.*" As we got out of the cab, I looked up at the museum and saw dozens of children milling about. The scene was just as I remembered it from thirty-five years earlier, when I first made the journey here on a class trip. I pulled myself out of the car, and we climbed the steps, winding our way through children sitting, talking, and eyeing one another's gift shop purchases. I felt a surge of strength and a lighter heart. I was here with my son, and joy skipped into my being once again as I gazed at his fresh young face.

A few weeks after our trip to the museum, we reached a major milestone in our lives: it was time for Tyler to start nursery school. As his first day drew near, I became quite apprehensive about how this transition might affect both Tyler and me. I had been going with him to the playground very infrequently, and if Joyce organized a play date for him, I encouraged her to have it at the friend's house. Now that we would be joining a school and the community that revolved around it, how would his classmates and their parents respond to me? I was concerned about scaring the other toddlers; I didn't want Tyler to have that mom kids are afraid of.

When the big day finally came, Greg and I walked him to the school. Tyler was over the moon with excitement. I was so proud, but also anxious, and I remember wearing white jeans, a red shirt, a sweater, and a sun hat to shade my face. Tyler wasn't anxious at all: he walked into the classroom, turned around, and said, "Bye, Mommy; bye, Daddy." We thought he might have paused a moment longer, but no, he was off like a shot.

A few nights later I was sitting in the living room admiring some of Tyler's artwork as he stood next to me. He had drawn a picture of Mommy, Daddy, and himself. Mommy was red, Daddy was pink, and he was green. I told him I liked the picture very much, and then he climbed up on the couch next to me and began examining a bandage on my finger that covered a recent infection.

"Don't worry," I said. "Mommy's going to be okay. Mommy's going to be just fine."

His expression serious, Tyler slid off the couch and looked up at me. He placed his hands on my knees and said, "Mommy, I'll make you feel better."

Smiling, I looked back at him and said, "You already have, more than you know."

That night I bent over my son as he lay in bed sleeping and then breathed in the smell of his skin and sweet breath. My aim had always been to restore my body so that I could be a full participant in my family's life. It was of the utmost importance to me that I in no way would become a further burden on my family. And I refused to be some dejected clunker. I couldn't bear the thought that Tyler might someday say, "Oh yes, that's my mother, you know . . . she's injured."

Here was where I would make my stand. "I am not going anywhere, baby," I whispered to Tyler. "I will be here for you always. We are not running away—this is our home. Don't you ever pay attention to what anyone says; you are a wonderful and amazing child, and your mama isn't going anywhere. I am just as strong and able as any other mother, and don't you ever forget it."

I kneeled down on the floor next to his bed and kissed his cheek and then his hand. Feeling as if I were praying at an altar, I bowed my head in thankfulness for all the happiness he'd already given me. This warm pulsating being was everything to me—my son, my friend, the future.

9

TURNING POINT

Life is like riding a bicycle—in order to keep your balance, you must keep moving.

—ALBERT EINSTEIN

When he was a young boy, my little brother Scot was as cute as can be. He had blond hair and blue eyes, and as his proud older sister I felt protective toward him. Six years separated us, but my sister and I often let him tag along as we made the neighborhood rounds. When it came time for him to learn to ride a bike and join the local posse, I appointed myself as his coach. At first, I pushed him along the curb and told him to drag his left foot on the ground for balance until he could find it on his own. Then, when I decided he'd had enough preparation, I declared, hands on hips, "Today, you will ride the bike yourself."

Standing beside him on the sidewalk in front of our house, I helped him get settled on his bike. "Just balance," I said, "like you're walking. You can do it, Scot."

Then I gave him a perfunctory push, and off he went. The sidewalk followed a small downgrade, so gravity aided his momentum.

He teetered and tottered, but somehow he remained vertical and began riding down the small hill.

"You did it!" I shouted.

"I did it!" he shouted back. By the time he neared the end of the sidewalk, he was picking up some real speed; in a wild scramble, he tumbled off the bike and landed in a heap in the grass as the bike shot into street.

Next time I would teach him how to brake.

During my recovery, I often felt like a child attempting to learn new skills. Teetering and tottering, toppling over, trying again—I was determined to do the same things everyone else could do.

My strength had returned in small increments. The daily changes were never pronounced, so I relished the monthly measurements of strength and agility that proved to my doctors and me that I was making progress. In what I sometimes called my previous life, I had been used to setting and achieving much bigger goals, and I could never have imagined that these small milestones would mean so much. By the spring of 2004, more than two and a half years after the attack, I needed only a profligate amount of petroleum jelly to soothe the areas of my skin that were cracked and raw; gone were the sterile pads I'd worn to control oozing from the areas that took the longest to heal, an accomplishment of which I was very proud. And though I wore my gloves and a mask at night, I no longer had to wear the full suit of pressure garments.

Because my dexterity and endurance were still so compromised, I continued to go to physical and occupational therapy five days a week. Its purpose was to restore my ranges of motion by forcibly breaking past the restrictions created by the internal and external scar tissue. The physical limits of one day became a wall to smash through the next, and pain was a constant. But a part of me continued to engage the pain: it helped me focus on the stiff, weak areas of my body and then attack them one by one.

In late spring, my therapists recommended that I decrease my in-hospital therapy to three times a week. I was excited to graduate, but fearful about losing any portion of my routine. Like training wheels, the weekday visits had provided comfort, consistency, and a place to go to "work." My OT, Lora Stubin-Amelio, and my PT, Malvina Sher, had become my coworkers and friends, and we often shared laughs and stories about one another's lives. Lora and Malvina continued to work with me after I cut back on my trips to the hospital, and it was gratifying to be able to spend so much more time at home.

With summer approaching, Greg felt strongly that I needed a real break. The previous two summers had felt especially claustrophobic, particularly because we had only escaped from the city for a couple of weeks. I was still emotionally exhausted from the regular and periodic surgeries, and since the house in Pine Plains needed work that would take months, Greg suggested that we return to Long Island for the summer.

"I think this would be good for you, good for us, and being near the ocean has always made you happy," he said.

How could I disagree?

The eastern end of Long Island has always held a special place in my heart. It speaks to me of light, beauty, and happiness, and whenever we pass over the Shinnecock Canal into Southampton, a feeling of contentment and peace descends upon me.

Just before Memorial Day, we picked up our bicycles, cobwebbed from four years of disuse, the gears a bit rusty and needing a tune-up. We loaded them onto the car and headed east; three hours later, just after passing the Milk Pail fruit and vegetable stand in Water Mill, we turned right onto Newlight Lane and then into the driveway of our summer rental. As I stepped out onto the gravel-packed driveway and felt the familiar crunch of rock under my feet, I let out a happy sigh of relief.

My great ambition for the weekend was to ride a bike for the first time in three years. Soon after we settled in, I decided that it was time for me to reckon with that chunk of metal waiting in the garage. Greg was excited about getting back out on the road with me, but I was secretly petrified. Trying to push away my fears, I imagined the worst that could happen. *Well,* I thought, *I could fall and perhaps lose a finger or two.* But then I chuckled, realizing that I had come close to accomplishing that without the bicycle. *What the hell,* I said to myself, *I've got to give it a whirl.*

I put my brain on reload, picked up my bicycle helmet, and told Greg that I was ready to go. After we wheeled the bikes out of the garage, Greg put my helmet on me and adjusted the straps.

While trying to mount the bicycle, I encountered a slight complication: the reach of my fingers wouldn't allow me to grip both the handlebar and the brake at the same time. Riding a bike would be that much more dangerous if I couldn't keep a couple of fingers on the brake, but there was nothing to be done about it. I would find a way to grab the brake or end up biting the dust.

I gripped the handlebar while Greg held the brake to keep the bicycle stationary. I swung my right leg over the seat and felt a few twinges of pain. As Greg helped hold the bike steady, I anchored my left foot to the pedal; because the scar bands on my left side ran the length of my body, this required a substantial downward push. "I'm all right," I said.

"Are you sure?" Greg asked.

"Absolutely."

"Okay, then—ready?"

I said yes and started peddling. After running beside me for a couple of steps, Greg gave me a little push and off I went. Greg hopped onto his bike and followed after me.

At first my pedaling was stiff and uncoordinated, and the bike wobbled precariously. But as I gathered speed, I steadied the bike and began to relax. I smiled and then started laughing with happiness. "I did it! Yay, I did it!" I shouted. As we coasted down Newlight Lane, Greg called out, "You're back!"

I was a woman who couldn't even dig inside my handbag without cutting a finger on a hairbrush or a change purse, but here I was riding a bike! The summer was off to a promising start.

That night, Greg and I danced at the ocean's edge, running along the surf and through the sequined water, the foam spraying us. Our clothes wet, we shivered in the cool early June night, laughing until we found ourselves crying with joy.

Before 9/11, I wasn't big on compromise. I wanted to be that superwoman who lived the "you can have it all and do it all" mantra that was so prevalent in the 1970s and '80s. Now, almost three years after my injury, I realized that many of the defeats I'd experienced were self-inflicted. Too often, I would chastise myself for small failures, thinking that I should have done better or done more. I was never satisfied with my success. I judged myself harshly, and as a result I had robbed myself of the happiness that should have been mine. I had lived at some level with a *Wizard of Oz* expectation that there really was someone behind the curtain who could make things right. But after losing control over my body and my life, I'd been forced to recognize that I needed to learn how to compromise and embrace even the little victories. Gradually, I let go of the absolutism and perfectionism that had plagued me for so long; now I felt at peace even if things didn't go exactly the way I wanted. It was a turning point in my life.

I had always dreamed of running in the New York City Marathon and racing through the streets of my beloved city. In June I was offered the opportunity to achieve a reasonable approximation of that goal, given my current circumstances: I was chosen to participate in the 2004 International Olympic Torch Relay, the first torch relay ever to span the entire globe. In advance of the Summer Games in Athens, the Olympic flame would travel from ancient Olympia, Greece, through every continent in the world, then back to Greece in a journey that would last seventy-eight days and cover thousands of miles. I was honored to be among those asked to carry the torch in a thirty-four-mile relay through the streets of New York.

Greg sent out an e-mail to our families and friends informing them that I would be carrying the Olympic flame as part of the New York City relay. Starting at 5:09 p.m. on Saturday, June 19, I would be running up Central Park West, from West Seventy-seventh Street to the north end of the American Museum of Natural History at Eightieth Street. Greg, my escort runner, would be by my side every step of the way.

A unique torch is designed for each session of the Olympics; in 2004, the design was inspired by the shape of an olive leaf, an appropriate model given the location of the games that year. The torch I would be carrying, I learned, was a beautiful tapered sculpture made of golden olive wood and magnesium with a matte silver finish. Like the other runners, I would receive my own torch to carry, and after the relay it would be mine to keep.

My torch and our uniforms arrived the night before the event. We opened the bag to find that Greg's clothes were too small, whereas mine were far too large. After trying them on, we looked so comical that we had to laugh at ourselves. Then we set about figuring out how to make the most of what we'd been sent. The elasticized cuffs on the pants and the logo design on the shirt made it impossible to cut the outfits down, and there simply wasn't time to perform any sort of complex tailoring.

Fortunately, Greg knew how to tie knots like a sailor, and several strategic knots and a few carefully inserted safety pins yielded the semblance of a uniform that fit me. Although I looked about twenty pounds heavier and displayed bulges in odd places, I felt pretty good about the outfit—after all, I was used to looking a bit different by now. My biggest fear was that the large pants would drop down around my ankles and I'd fall flat on the asphalt, the Olympic torch tumbling away across Central Park West.

The big day dawned sunny and hot, and I was concerned about how I would handle the heat. In the afternoon, we took a cab up to Chelsea Piers, where we joined the other runners in a large tented area. Hundreds of people milled about, buzzing excitedly. Standing there, I remembered my last visit to the Museum of Natural History; that memorable trip with Tyler was one of the first times I had ventured out with my son alone. I was as anxious now as I had been then.

The relay coordinator gave everyone the necessary instructions: how far each of us would carry the torch; how far we needed to stay behind the lead car; and, most important, how to light the torch of the next runner. This last bit worried me. Small butane containers were lodged inside the slim torches, and to receive the flame I would need to twist the base of the torch to release the fuel and then hope the relay runner before me would dip his or her torch at the correct angle toward mine and thus ignite it. I also wondered whether I would be able to hold the torch high and steadily enough to light the next runner's torch without dropping my own. As the time for departure approached, I repeatedly practiced the necessary motions.

Once we all had our orders, we crossed to a long line of waiting buses that would take runners to different points along the relay route. As we began our journey uptown, we flung the windows open and shouted out to the crowds and the other buses of departing runners, wishing them luck and cheering them on. Soon we reached my starting point on Central Park West, and my heart skipped a beat as we stepped off the bus. A large crowd lined the street, and I heard people call out, "Go USA! Go USA! Go Lauren!" My parents, along with Tyler, Gigi, Laura, and Bert, had taken their positions on the museum's steps, while other friends greeted us at the starting point. The relay route was closed to vehicles, and the wide expanse of Central Park West—flanked on the east by Central Park and on the west by ornate prewar buildings, most especially the museum—resembled a grand European boulevard. While we waited on the east side of the intersection at Seventy-seventh Street for the Olympic flame to arrive, the crowd shouted and cheered.

Right on schedule, the pace vehicle—a small truck filled with camera operators and photographers—came up the street. As soon as it passed, I stepped out to await the runner's arrival. I twisted the base of my torch to release the fuel and then lifted my torch, higher than I thought I could. Suddenly the runner was there. I reached upward, stretching, and held the tip of my torch to his— and nothing happened. But after a few seconds that felt like forever, the flame finally caught.

I turned, and then Greg and I were off. It wasn't easy for me to hold the torch aloft, even though it had a narrow base. The flame swayed back and forth as I ran, and unlike the other runners who held it up and to the side, Lady Liberty style, I had to hold the torch with two hands to keep from dropping it. As a result, the flame was directly in front of me, just an arm's length away. I felt the heat and feared my hair would catch fire, but I forged on.

As we ran behind the truck, Greg and I looked from side to side as people called out and cheered us on. We spotted Gigi, Laura, and Bert waving and shouting our names. On the steps of the museum, my mom was holding Tyler up in her arms, and I heard him call out, "Mommy, Mommy, you're a good runner!"

At the end of my route I held up my torch to ignite the flame for the next runner. The exchange went flawlessly, and the flame continued on its way north up Central Park West in the late afternoon sun. That night we attended a reception held by Mayor Michael Bloomberg at Gracie Mansion to celebrate the event.

The next morning Greg opened the Sunday *New York Times*, and there at the bottom of the front page was a photograph of the two of us running the relay, with me holding the torch in front of me and smiling. I look genuinely happy; my smile is wide, and my face is filled with a look of wonder. Running next to me, Greg is smiling just as broadly.

That Saturday I brought the torch I had carried to the house on Newlight Lane. We had our first guests of the summer that weekend, and it was the first time anyone but family had stayed with us since the summer of 2001. The barbecue was fired up, margaritas flowed, and by a mixture of porch lights, candlelight, and moonlight, Greg relighted the torch and we all took turns running our own mini-Olympic relay.

That I could run and ride again, albeit less fluidly than before, meant a great deal to me, because in so many ways my life would never be the same. Since my hands were significantly smaller and all my fingers except my right thumb had at least one joint fusion, I had to modify my approach to even the simplest things. I could no longer widen my fingers enough to lift most drinking glasses with a single hand, so I resorted to a two-handed grip. My hand-writing, which wasn't particularly good before, was now almost illegible, and half the time I couldn't even read what I'd written. But at least I could still type, though more slowly and more pain-fully than before.

Ultimately I realized that I could accomplish many of the same tasks, but only by adapting. Years of stretching and strengthening had allowed me not just to walk but to run, lift weights, and even-tually even do push-ups on my knuckles. But these were little more than first steps if I wanted to play catch with Tyler and return to playing sports, so the next task was to rebuild my athletic capa-bilities. Despite considerable progress, I still confronted serious restrictions in my ranges of movement, so relearning how to play tennis or golf brought new challenges and risks. And my most serious competition would not be provided by an opponent; in the end, I would really be competing with myself.

By late 2004, we'd become so attached to the eastern end of Long Island that we'd reluctantly decided to sell the house in Pine Plains. In December, with the help of Liz Clarke, a broker in South-ampton who'd become a good friend, we bought a weathered, cedar-shingle house in Sagaponack. We moved in the following Memorial Day, and one morning early that summer I decided it was time to see if I could manage to play a game of catch with Tyler. Now four and a half years old, Tyler already showed signs of being a good athlete, and as he and I stood on the lawn and prepared to throw a youth baseball back and forth, I realized that it would be a learning experience for both of us.

Sure enough, when Tyler threw the ball to me and I caught it, he said, "You caught it! Nice catch, Mom."

"Of course I can catch," I said. "I used to play on a softball team."

"I know, Mom. But you're really good, especially for an injured mom."

"Thanks, buddy."

But if Tyler was confident about his ability to throw and catch a ball, he was still a little intimidated by the prospect of riding a bicycle. The previous summer, he had mastered the trick of riding a bike with training wheels, and he had spent a lot of time barreling down the street at breakneck speed, the *whrrrrrr* of the small plastic wheels singing on the macadam.

Now, after persuading Greg to remove his training wheels, he tried to ride his bike without them. But no matter how much we helped him, he fell—over and over again. His knees scraped and his confidence injured, he abandoned his efforts for a time. His bike sat in the garage, a lonely reminder of failure, and when the other children pedaled down the block, smiles on their faces, Tyler would watch them longingly. But if I suggested he try again, he would refuse.

"I'll try again, Mom. Just not right now."

"Okay, Ty, whenever you're ready."

"I just don't want to get hurt, Mom. I don't want to have pain; I don't want my blood to come out."

Here was my tough little guy, lean and strong and capable, grappling with his fear and his knowledge of how bad an injury can be. Finally I persuaded him to try riding his bike on the lawn, telling him that if he fell he wouldn't get hurt because he'd land on grass.

It was a warm day in July. I was barefoot and, improbably, wearing a flowing white cotton summer dress. Tyler straddled his bicycle at the far end of the lawn, his helmet on, and I stood alongside him, gripping one handlebar and the back of his seat so he could mount up. As he looked at the lawn stretching before him, Tyler's face showed only fear.

We started to move. "Mom, not too fast!" he said.

"No worries about that, Ty."

The drag of the grass allowed him to go forward in relative slow motion, and before he knew it, he was riding on his own. Just before the hedge line, he tumbled off, unhurt.

He lifted himself up off the grass, his eyes wide. "I did it, Mom. I can ride a bike!"

I ran over to him and hugged him, so proud of his courage to try again.

Next time we would work on braking.

Another high point of the summer of 2005 was the Cantor Fitzgerald Relief Fund White Party. Organized by Edie Lutnick and now in its third year, the White Party was a beachfront clambake that honored the memory of Gary Lutnick and benefited the children of the Cantor Fitzgerald employees lost on 9/11. Eager to support the event, Greg and I donated performances by Christine Gordon—the singer who had organized so many meals at the Burn Center—and the Rolling Bones, and I became one of the event's cochairs.

That year's event was a great success. After Christine's set ended and as the Bones were preparing to play, I stepped away from the party for a few minutes and walked by myself up a path flanked by sea grass to the top of a dune. Feeling the sand between my toes and a cool breeze against my back, I looked up at the stars and then down at all the partygoers dressed in white. The gathering looked so small against the black expanse of the ocean, but the warmth of the lights and the laughter beckoned me. For a moment I realized that I was once again apart, but this time it was by my own choice. I watched the party for a minute or two longer and then, just before returning, said aloud, "I am still one of you."

In the waning days of August, a group of friends and I decided to host an end-of-summer clambake of our own.

It was another beautiful evening, and as the caterer kindled a fire in a cast-iron firepot that was buried level with the sand, our guests gathered for drinks and a celebration of the joys of summer. After a delicious dinner of lobster and grilled chicken, we all stood by the sunset bonfire and watched the surf breaking onto the beach just thirty feet away. Finally, when only a few guests and their children remained, two men from the catering company used metal rods to lift the firepot and carry it toward the water, with Greg walking behind and making sure that the kids remained a safe distance away. The caterers turned the firepot over and dumped its contents into the waves, where the fire died in a hiss of steam.

I was saying good night to one of the remaining couples when we heard Tyler and their daughter screaming. We turned and ran over to them. Tyler was rolling on his back in the sand, holding his left leg, crying, "Help, Mommy! It hurts, it hurts!"

I bent down and pulled him into my arms, saying, "It'll be all right, honey."

While chasing each other, Tyler and his friend had run into the unmarked hole left by the firepot and planted their bare feet in sand that had been heated to well over five hundred degrees. Though she was crying, the girl was all right; but Tyler wasn't as fortunate.

Greg sprinted to get the car as I carried Tyler, still crying out in pain, off the beach. As I labored to run through the soft sand, my legs felt leaden and the parking lot seemed miles away. Finally I put Tyler into the car, and we sped off toward Southampton Hospital.

Entering the ER, I felt a familiar dread. The nurses in their brightly colored tops sat at reception; the smell of antiseptic blended with the matted scent of cotton; the shiny linoleum tile floor gave our footsteps a hollow, clacking sound. Everywhere I saw and heard and smelled reminders of my sickly past.

The triage nurse ushered us into an examination room, and a young doctor came in and examined Tyler.

"He has a second-degree burn on the front of his left ankle, but his toes will be okay," he said, looking down at Tyler's foot. "The wound will heal on its own, but for the next couple of weeks, he can't wear any shoes or socks, and you have to take care of the burn."

"What do we need to do for it?" Greg asked.

"Well, it's summer. Let him run around barefoot, and he can go swimming as often as he wants. In fact, the water will help with debridement, which is—"

"I'm familiar with it," I said, interrupting him politely.

The doctor looked up at me for a moment and realized that I knew all about debridement.

"Okay, so you know what I mean," he continued. "Twice a day, you'll need to take some gauze and very lightly scrub the burn site with soap and water."

It was a blessing that Tyler's injury hadn't been worse. But no matter how gentle we tried to be, I knew how much the burn would hurt, and it broke my heart to think that my son, not yet five years old, would have to endure even this small part of what I had gone through.

Every morning and evening for the next ten days, Greg and I set Tyler down on the bathroom vanity, put his left foot in the sink, and washed the burn site. At the beginning of the first session, Greg scrubbed the burn as lightly as he could, but the pain made it very hard for Tyler to hold still.

"Tyler, you have to let me do this, or the burn won't heal," Greg told him patiently. "You can cry. I know it hurts. But you have to hold your leg still. Be tough, like your mom."

"Okay, Daddy," Tyler said.

As Greg washed the burn, tears flowed down Tyler's face, but his small leg never moved.

The wound healed successfully, and one day Tyler asked if he needed to go to the sink again.

"No, honey, you're all done!" I said.

"Mommy, it hurt, and I cried," Tyler said. "But I did what I had to do, and I took it, just like you did."

10

NIGHT RIDER

Where there is great love there are always miracles.

—WILLA CATHER

In October 2005, Tyler turned five years old. He was a caring, well-liked kid with amber eyes and sun-streaked blond hair. Greg and I agreed that he was unusually self-assured for his age; he seemed to understand instinctively how important it was to be true to himself, perhaps because he'd had to come to terms with what had happened to me. And although he was intrepid and almost always cheerful, he carried his own scars from the years after 9/11.

He was now old enough to understand that terrorists had attacked the World Trade Center. He had seen an appearance of ours on the *Today Show* that included footage from 9/11, and especially after learning about the Madrid train bombings in March 2004 and the London train bombings in July 2005, he knew that our country might be the target of another attack by terrorists. Sometimes, in quiet moments, he would ask me when the terrorists were coming back. He would also ask me why more people weren't saved on 9/11. The monsters he feared weren't under his bed; when he spoke to me about how I'd been injured or about his own memories of the past few years, his monsters were real. Greg and I told him that nothing like 9/11 would ever happen to him; then we prayed that we were right. We did our best to help him keep his balance, to remain a happy and hopeful kid.

Though Tyler didn't speak often about his fears of another attack, he did talk all the time about wanting a sibling. In fact, he would turn to just about anyone and say, "I keep telling my mom and dad that I want a brother or sister, but I don't see them doing anything about it."

What Tyler didn't know was that I wanted him to have a sibling more than just about anything else. It had always been my plan to have more than one child, and sometimes I would look at my son and mourn the absence of the brother or sister who should have been beside him. I couldn't bear the thought that the terrorists might have taken away my opportunity to be a mother again, and from the beginning of my recovery, I had insisted that someday I would try to have another child.

Only now, in late 2005, did I begin to believe that my body was ready for the stresses of pregnancy. And although at age forty-three I faced even more daunting odds, Dr. Michael Silverstein, the obstetrician who had delivered Tyler, told me there was no reason why I couldn't or shouldn't try to get pregnant.

A couple of weeks later, Greg and I returned to the familiar waiting room at the NYU Fertility Center to consult with Dr. Frederick Licciardi, the same doctor who had helped us so much when we were trying to have Tyler. He ran the requisite hormone tests and confirmed that I could try again. After undergoing another unrelated surgery that winter, I commenced my first post-9/11 IVF cycle in April 2006.

Gonadotropin, estradiol, and progesterone were back in the refrigerator. This time the daily injections hurt more, because the needle had to push through tender skin in some places and thickened, scarred tissue in other areas. I willed my body to cooperate, but it rebelled. Though Dr. Licciardi was able to harvest a number of viable eggs, the lining of my uterus didn't thicken sufficiently, and with no place for the eggs to adhere, implantation wasn't possible. We tried again in May but encountered the same problem. In June, my lining achieved the lowest acceptable thickness, and Dr. Licciardi implanted three beautiful embryos. I was buoyed by high doses of progesterone, and Greg and I prayed that the fates and good luck would visit us. On day nine I had my blood drawn and then boarded a shuttle bus out to eastern Long Island and our house in Sagaponack to await the results. About two hours later, my cell phone vibrated. Seeing that the call was from NYU/IVF, I voiced a barely audible prayer—"Please God, please"—and answered the call.

It was one of the nurses. "I am so sorry, Mrs. Manning," she said. "I'm afraid the numbers aren't good."

I choked out a cursory thank-you and hung up. Settling back in my seat, I looked out the window. Tears pooled in the corners of my eyes; I felt emptied, both physically and emotionally.

Soon the bus passed through the Long Island Pine Barrens. In 1995, long stretches on both sides of the highway had burned in a huge wildfire, and the flames had left behind a postapocalyptic landscape of charred stumps and blasted trees. Now, a decade later, thousands of seedlings were rising among the blackened skeletons, forming a thick carpet of dark green. *Even the Pine Barrens are no longer barren*, I thought to myself. *How is it that I am unable to have another child? How could I have failed at a task that was so much easier than surviving the fires I'd endured?* The doctors had assured me that I could carry a healthy embryo to term, but perhaps my body—speaking to me again, as it had through the stomach demon years before—was telling me that this was one thing it could no longer do.

The highway narrowed to two lanes soon after we crossed the Shinnecock Canal. But this time, instead of contentment and peace, the trip across the bridge had brought only sadness and pain.

Over the next few weeks Dr. Licciardi ran a new series of tests, but the results were inconclusive. In September, he officially diagnosed me as having "unexplained infertility."

"If you really want to build your family and you're comfortable with it, you should consider using a gestational carrier," Dr. Licciardi told us. A surrogate mother, he explained, typically contributes the egg for the embryo she is carrying, whereas a gestational carrier or gestational surrogate would carry to term an embryo made entirely from our genetic material.

When we'd first returned to see Dr. Licciardi, Greg and I had felt optimistic that we would soon be the proud parents of a new baby. Now it was gradually becoming clear that if Tyler were ever to have a sibling, we would have to undertake an entirely new odyssey. Disheartened but still determined, we entered a new phase in our quest.

We began by getting in touch with a consultant in California. But after months of effort to find an appropriate gestational surrogate through her, we came to another heartbreaking dead end. Next, after hearing good things about an organization called the Center for Surrogate Parenting, or CSP, we traveled to Annapolis,

Maryland, to interview its administrative team and the woman who would be our coordinator and facilitator. During the meeting, we learned that we would be matched with a carefully chosen surrogate whom we would meet in person before we agreed to proceed, and that CSP's staff would support both us and the surrogate throughout the experience. It was a very positive meeting, and we left feeling hopeful for the first time in months.

But after being matched with a fine surrogate, we once again came up short. Over the next year, three promising attempts at pregnancy failed, and finally the surrogate was no longer able to continue. Still determined to go forward, we went back to CSP, and in the spring of 2007 our coordinator introduced us to a second surrogate, an extraordinary woman from Florida named Juliet Jones.

We had been through so much by now that we had lost nearly all of our early optimism. But Juliet's confidence brought us back to a place of hope. The mother of two wonderful boys, she had a generous smile and an infectious laugh, and she naturally put us at ease. She lived in a town called Celebration, worked for Disney, and was terrifically responsible and well organized. Most important, she had been a surrogate before and had successfully delivered twins.

Greg and I couldn't envision a better match. After our meeting with Juliet, I thought of the Disney theme song, which had suddenly acquired new meaning.

What I desired most in my heart might finally be coming to me.

Once again we stepped onto the treadmill of IVF cycles. In August a promising cycle ultimately came to naught; in November, another cycle with Juliet also proved unsuccessful. This time I reacted not just with disappointment and sadness, but with the self-condemnation that greets repeated failure. Juliet's inability to become pregnant after being implanted with my fertilized eggs must be my fault; since she'd been so successful in the past, what else could it be? Now, facing what seemed to be very long odds, Greg and I groped for reasons to persevere and came close to abandoning the surrogacy process for good.

In early January 2008, we decided to pursue one last cycle with Juliet. She, and we, deserved one more chance. If we were successful, then that was meant to be. If this last attempt failed, we would console ourselves with the knowledge that we already had one perfect child and leave it at that.

Toward the end of the month, Greg and I received word that, unbelievably, Juliet was pregnant. Experience had taught us to temper our expectations, but we felt a glimmer of hope. Two and a half months later, we flew down to Orlando, Florida, to be with Juliet for an appointment during which she would have the second-trimester ultrasound and undergo amniocentesis. During the sonogram, Greg and I held hands and looked at the image on the screen, overwhelmed by the thought that we would finally be having another baby.

A few days later, when the initial results came back from the amniocentesis, we were told that everything looked fine, but that some additional tests of the amniotic fluid needed to be performed. A week after that, the doctor called to tell us that some of the test results were unusual, and while he didn't believe that we were dealing with a major problem, he recommended genetic counseling.

This sounded ominous, but we tried to remain optimistic. We

made an appointment at a genetic counseling center in New York and brought in the report. There we were told that the results presented a significant issue. When a second opinion confirmed this conclusion, we were thrown into a tailspin. Before us now lay the agonizing decision whether to terminate the pregnancy. Just at the moment when we should have been preparing a place for Tyler's sibling in our home and our hearts, we faced yet more emptiness and pain. We couldn't help feeling that our game of defying the odds was up and that fate had won.

The choice not to allow the pregnancy to continue seemed clear, but it was devastating to make. Greg and I felt a crushing sadness. We had tried over and over to have another child, yet we had failed. Despite all I'd been through, I don't think I had ever experienced a feeling of such utter defeat.

I also felt terrible that Juliet had to endure a pain that should have been mine. Yet when we told Juliet of our decision, she understood. She wrote us a lovely, comforting e-mail; then, during a conversation on the phone a few weeks later, she told me she was willing to try again. But for the first time, I admitted that I wasn't sure I could go through the cycle of hope and failure again.

"It has been such a burden for so long, and I am so tired," I told her. "I just don't know if I still believe that it will happen. I used to be sure, but I'm not sure anymore. And I don't see how I can ask any more from you."

There was a momentary pause, and then Juliet spoke. "Lauren, you have been through so much, but you never stopped trying. You didn't quit, and I'm not going to quit on you. I want you and Greg to have this baby."

Close to tears, I could barely speak. She wanted this baby for us: she was determined to see it born. Her generosity was beyond measure, and to know that I had inspired her to continue to make the effort was overwhelming.

"Thank you, Juliet," I said. "Thank you."

Months later, when Juliet was ready, we tried one last time. It was February 2009, more than three years since I had first dared to hope for another child. We knew that if we failed this time, there would be no more attempts. No matter the outcome, this would be the last play of the game. It was time to throw our "Hail Mary" pass, or, as Juliet called it, "Hail Manning."

I had been disappointed so many times before that I didn't even mark the day the pregnancy test results were due. When they came in positive, I was almost nonplussed. Greg, Juliet, and I had a subdued conversation that evening; like veterans who had seen too many tours, we all agreed that we would just take it a day at a time. We had such a long way to go, and we knew that many things could still go wrong.

Three weeks later, though, Juliet had her first ultrasound and reported positive news. "I actually heard the heartbeat, which the doctor said was excellent given that it's still pretty early in the process," Juliet said. "But no matter where we are, that *lub-dub* is a lovely sound."

She e-mailed us an image of the fetus from the ultrasound, and I wrote back, "One can build a mountain from a single grain of sand—especially such a cute grain of sand!"

Still, Greg and I remained apprehensive, and in June we flew to Florida for Juliet's amniocentesis and second-trimester ultra-sound. We were completely neutral when we entered the exam room to meet with the doctor; after so many disappointments, we refused to look beyond the day's results. But the ultrasound—

which revealed that Juliet was carrying a baby boy—suggested that the pregnancy was proceeding normally, and the amniocentesis results were normal. Cautiously, we allowed a ray of hope to reenter our hearts.

By late June, Juliet had been pregnant for almost five months. For fear that it would tip the scales of fate against us, we hadn't yet told anyone about the pregnancy. If things did go wrong, we didn't want to share the sadness of a final failure. But at last we began to believe that we really would be having a second child.

Tyler had never stopped demanding a sibling, and although he would have been happy with a sister, he had always spoken of having a baby brother. Finally he would get his wish, although telling him so would be a bit complicated, because we would need to explain that his brother was, for now, the guest of a gestational carrier. Still, the time had come to give him the joyful news, and I decided that the announcement called for something special.

I had often thought it would be great fun to take Tyler on a grand adventure, but we'd never had the right opportunity. True, we had visited faraway friends and vacation destinations, but other than trips to Williamsburg and Washington, DC, we had not traveled to a place that had its own rich history. Tyler would turn nine years old in the fall, and the three of us had lived through almost a decade of joy, tragedy, and rebuilding. Now, before the arrival of a new baby, was the perfect moment for all of us to take a trip together. After discussing several possible destinations, Greg and I decided we would visit Italy and break the big news to Tyler in Rome.

On July 18, we flew to Venice, where, after landing, we rode the polished teak water taxi across the Laguna Veneta and into the city. That first night, we hired a gondola and floated down the Grand Canal at sunset. As we passed under the Rialto Bridge, the gondolier instructed Greg in accented English, "Sir, kiss your wife." Tradition has it that those who kiss while passing beneath the bridge at sunset are assured eternal love. I kissed Greg and then hugged Tyler and gave him a kiss as well.

Three days later we traveled to Florence. Tyler, showing a keen sense for Italian fashion, led us into a Foot Locker on Via dei Calzaiuoli. He wanted to buy a pair of European Nikes, but he also had his heart set on buying a tiny pair of sneakers in case he ever had a little brother or sister. Had the outcome of our latest cycle been otherwise, this would have been a painful moment. Instead, Greg and I smiled at each other and agreed that Tyler could buy the smallest pair of navy blue, light-up Geox.

On July 25 we arrived in Rome, our final destination. Ever since landing in Venice, I'd been feeling like a child with a big secret, knowing that after so much pain and hard work the miraculous event was fast approaching. When I was pregnant with Tyler, I'd felt his every kick and hiccup, but this time there was no outward sign that our new baby was on his way. This time, our precious being was traveling toward us through time on what Greg called his little "business trip," and for the moment my second son and I were separated by the Mediterranean and the Atlantic.

On the afternoon of our first day in Rome, we left our hotel and headed for the Trevi Fountain. We turned a corner, and there it was, rising before us. Eighty-five feet high and more than sixty feet wide, the fountain is a sculpture of free-flowing rock in the shape of giant waves. A great statue of Ocean presides, as his Tritons tame the wild Hippocampi and other statues pay homage to abundance, energy, fertility, and plenty. The fountain's name is derived from the Latin word *trivium*, which means "three ways," and I immediately thought of the long roads that each of the three of us had traveled to reach this place of wishes and dreams.

Crowds of people were seated all along the fountain's edge. We found a bit of open space at the west end, and Tyler and I took a seat. Greg and I had brought a few coins for our wish making, and we gave the first one to Tyler. He took it and immediately made the motion of throwing it over his shoulder. Then, wearing a mischievous expression, he brought his arm down and showed us that he still had the coin in his hand.

After I told him to be sure to make a wish, Tyler turned away from the fountain and tossed the coin over his shoulder into the water. He asked for a second coin and again threw it over his shoulder, at which point I announced that I wanted to make a wish too. Smiling, I sat for a moment at the fountain's edge and then tossed my coin over my right shoulder into the fountain.

Finally the moment had come to tell Tyler why we were there.

"Daddy and I want to tell you something, Tyler," I began. "Are you ready?"

I paused for a moment as Tyler looked at me a bit warily.

"You know how you make wishes and sometimes they come true?" I said.

Tyler slowly nodded.

"Well, guess what? You're going to have a baby brother."

Tyler looked at me with a sidelong glance, surprised but wanting very much to believe.

I nodded and with a big smile said again, "You're going to have a baby brother!"

"How do you know?" Tyler asked, and Greg and I both laughed at the one response neither of us had expected.

"How do I know?" I said. "Because your daddy and I are the parents."

Tyler paused for a beat and looked straight at me, his eyes wide. Then his face lit up with a blazing smile, and he clapped his hands together in celebration.

"Now there's only one little thing we need to tell you, Tyler," I continued. "Remember Juliet, that wonderful lady we met? Because I was injured, it wasn't so easy for me to get pregnant, so she's carrying your baby brother. He's a passenger in her tummy, but he's your baby brother. He's going to be born November 6."

"Wait," Tyler said, his voice excited. "What day is it?"

"July 25," I said. "It's almost August."

"I can't wait!" he said.

Greg reminded him of the shoes he'd bought a few days earlier.

"I bought light-up shoes for my baby brother!" Tyler practically yelled. Giving me a big hug, he said, "I cannot wait."

"Can you believe it?" I said. "Wishes can come true, Tyler. He's coming just a few days after your birthday."

"I'll be nine."

"And you'll be his big brother."

For a moment Tyler looked away toward the fountain. "But he'll be adopted, right?"

"No, no, no—he's your blood," I told him. "Mommy and Daddy's blood too. Juliet, wonderful Juliet, is carrying him in her tummy for us."

"She put him in her tummy," he said, asking the question as a statement, tapping his fingertips against his own stomach, trying to piece these facts together.

"Our egg, inside of her, grew, and that's where he is right now. But he's your blood."

"You're going to have a baby brother," Greg said.

"Do you want to say, 'Thank you, Juliet'?" I asked Tyler.

"Thank you, Juliet!" Tyler shouted. "You are the most awesome person ever!"

An hour or two later, we visited the Piazza Navona, where we had dinner at one of the outdoor cafés. Wearing his soccer jersey, Tyler posed proudly with his fork placed in the center of a mountain of spaghetti, the newest of Rome's triumphant figures.

"I love Rome," Tyler said. "Don't you? This was the best day of my life."

The following evening we had a delicious dinner at the Eden Roc, one of Rome's great hotels. While eating, we watched another glorious sunset over the city, followed by a fireworks show in the distance against the background of Michelangelo's dome at Saint Peter's Basilica.

While Tyler was off reviewing the dessert tray, I turned to Greg. "Why did you stay with me?" I asked him. "Why didn't you move on?"

He brushed his hand against my cheek and said, "That's easy, Lauren. I knew I already had everything I ever really wanted."

October 22, 2009, was a balmy fall day, full of sun and blue skies. Greg and I were walking south down Fifth Avenue, opposite Central Park, when my cell phone rang. It was about 2:30 p.m.

"Lauren, hi, it's Juliet. I've gone into labor. They're going to deliver my passenger tonight!"

Hearing Juliet's words, I suddenly felt outside of myself, as if I were watching a movie about someone else and couldn't quite believe there would be a happy ending. But no, this was real—the arrival of our new baby boy, Jagger, was finally happening.

Originally we'd planned to fly to Florida on November 6, Jagger's due date, but now we needed to be on the next plane to

Orlando in order to get there in time for Jagger's birth. Gigi had gotten engaged over the summer, and this unexpectedly early trip south meant that we would miss her wedding, though Tyler would still represent us as the ring bearer. It was sad to think that I'd miss her big day, but I knew she would understand.

As we walked, I got back on my cell and booked the last two seats on the 5:30 p.m. Delta flight from LaGuardia to Orlando. Less than three hours later, we were seated on the starboard side of the plane as it took off. While looking to the west at a brilliant orange and rose sunset, we listened to Oscar Peterson and Count Basie's "Night Rider" on Greg's iPod. The song, an extended jazz jam, gathers and builds for more than ten minutes as the Night Rider approaches his destination. And as we approached ours, a void in my heart began to fill, and a long-ago sadness began to recede into oblivion. On that flight, "Night Rider" became Jagger's theme song—every time we hear it, we are soaring to meet him again.

Normally thronged with passengers, Orlando International Airport was nearly empty when we landed just past eight o'clock. Minutes mattered if we were to be there for Jagger's arrival, so we ran to pick up our rental car. As we did, we received a message from Juliet saying that the doctor had decided he couldn't wait any longer and was starting the C-section. Once in the car, I drove while Greg navigated, and together we raced the minutes down. Finally we pulled under the hospital's port cochere, parked right in front of the No Parking sign, and ran into the hospital.

We rode the elevator up to the maternity floor; hurrying down the long, quiet hallway, I felt as if I could hear my heart pounding. We rang the intercom and were buzzed in. When we approached two nurses sitting at their station, it was 9:47 p.m.

"We're looking for Jagger Manning," Greg said. "Is he here yet?"

"He's here," said a doctor who was sitting nearby.

"When?"

"Five minutes ago: 9:42 p.m. Congratulations."

One of the nurses smiled and said she would bring us to the delivery room. We washed our hands, donned yellow gowns and surgical masks, and then the nurse led us into the room. Lying on a white quilted sheet under a heat lamp, wearing a blue cap, was Jagger Thomas Manning, five minutes old.

I bent over him, smiled, and touched his cap with my left hand. "Welcome to the world, my sweetheart," I said. "We love you. Mom and Dad are here to take you home."

I took his left hand in my right, and he curled his fingers around my thumb.

Turning, Greg and I saw Juliet lying beneath surgical drapes. We could see only her head and the exhausted but beaming smile on her face.

"Juliet, how can we ever thank you?" I said. "You are amazing— thank you, thank you, thank you."

Minutes later, after moving to our designated birthing room, I held my newborn son in my arms and gave him his first bottle. Naturally there was a Yankees playoff game on the room's television; as always during the birth of my sons, the Yankees were on the march to a World Series championship. This year's title would be their first since the night Tyler was born.

Greg and I held each other, looking down at Jagger.

"You never stopped trying, Lauren," Greg said.

"I couldn't stop trying," I said. "I promised him I would find him."

Greg and I took turns giving Jagger his bottle through the

night, and I slept for a while with our beautiful baby boy nestled beside me. From time to time, I would open my eyes to gaze at our miracle, and to make sure, as mothers do, that he was breathing. Brushing my cheek against his head, I felt the weight of his small, warm body. *How*, I wondered, *can he be so fragile, yet so full of life?*

Lying there, I marveled at this new beginning. Jagger brought us back to a world of innocence and trust, one that had been taken away from us when Tyler was ten months old. This time, I would be there for my son's first steps and for his first birthday. I held in my arms the great gift that ended a quest that had lasted for more than eight years. A great wave of love poured through my being and into his; our spirits were forever bound together, sealed with the will to live.

On October 26, the day before Tyler's birthday, we brought his baby brother home. We couldn't possibly have conceived a better birthday gift. Tyler welcomed us at the door, saying, "He's so little!"

My mother embraced me, and she said. "Oh, Lauren, Lauren, he's here. He's finally here." Behind her, my father said, "Well done!"

Tyler sat down, and I gently placed Jagger in his arms. He looked down at his little brother tenderly, kissed him on the forehead, and said, "Welcome home, Jagger."

It wasn't just Jagger who was home. We all were.

THE WAY HOME

The soul's dominion? Each time we make a choice, we pay with
courage to behold restless day and count it fair.

—AMELIA EARHART

About a month before we brought Jagger home, Greg and I spent
a rainy afternoon going through some boxes we'd stored in the
basement of our house in Sagaponack. One of these was a large
clothing box, three feet on a side, with LAUREN scrawled across
the top. I peeled back the tape and pulled open the flaps, and in
the glow cast by a naked sixty-watt lightbulb hanging from the
ceiling I peered inside and then instantly recoiled in fear.

Gasping, physically shaken, I took a moment to collect myself
and understand what I'd seen.

Lying on top of folded stacks of flesh-colored pressure garments that almost completely filled the large box were eight or nine
clear plastic masks, tribal totems staring up at me with ghastly
empty eye sockets. As the contours of my face had changed, the
compression masks I'd worn had been refitted, and the box was
filled with the layers I'd molted as I'd healed. With every step

forward I had exchanged one confining prison for another, each tighter than the last.

I shuddered and pushed the box away, as shocked at the force of memory as I was by its distance.

"Let's burn it," I said.

In the summer of 2010, Greg and I spent an evening with two close friends of ours, Cheri and Michael Friedman. Cheri and I had met in 2004, when we took our sons to their first summer play class at Hayground Country Day Camp. Over dinner, Cheri and I reminisced about that summer and talked about how much our boys had grown, and then she said something that caught me completely by surprise.

"Lauren, you've changed so much since 2004," she said. "You weren't very well when we first came to know one another."

I was taken aback. I remembered feeling almost triumphant the summer Cheri and I met. I was going out in public. I was taking my son to day camp. I was participating in everyday life. I thought I was already so much better. Wasn't I?

A few days after our dinner, I came across a photograph from that summer. In it, I am sitting in the backyard of our house, holding three-year-old Tyler on my knee. Behind us, a deep pink and orange sunset fills the horizon. Tyler and I are both smiling; he appears to be giggling. It is a joyful photo, and I am obviously elated to have my son in my arms.

But now, looking at the photo six years later, I was amazed at my appearance. The skin of my left arm is raised and reddened with scars, the muscles thin with atrophy. A tight scar band stretches from my chin to my collarbone, and because of a deficit of skin on the left side of my neck, my lower lip is pulled down and to the left. A crescent-shaped scar lines my mouth directly beneath my lower lip, as thick and wide as the lip itself.

The face that stared back at me from that snapshot was virtually a stranger—an injured stranger very much in love with her son, a woman who would, step-by-step, become me. Sitting there, smiling and happy, she had no idea how far she had to go. I felt so sad for her, but also, so proud.

My metamorphosis required determination, strength, and resilience. I willed myself to look past my circumstances; projecting confidence, I hoped to persuade other people to participate in my charade. I would be so present, so forthright, so convincingly unharmed that when people met me they wouldn't notice any scars. They would not see a terribly injured person.

At some point over the past decade, the charade became reality and the injured woman disappeared. I can't imagine having to face those years again. The days and nights of pain and sadness carried me slowly through the years, but now they are almost gone. I have reached a separate peace with the person I have become. The ghosts of those who were lost haunt me now with memories of happiness and laughter, for that is how I choose to remember them.

Once you have been burned alive, you forever understand the small vanities that we humans live by. The injury I suffered was perhaps more intimate than any other; it was all-encompassing, from the outside in, but it never conquered me. With each step of my recovery, I learned that I am not just a carcass, that the shell encasing me is not my real beauty. I learned this when my mother hugged me with no thought except how much she loved me; when Greg smiled at me and reached out to hold me; when Tyler called out, "Mommy!" and came running over to give me an Eskimo kiss.

We look in the mirror to see our reflection, but the real reflection is the inner mirror that we hold to ourselves, the one that tells us the truth of who we really are. The body I saw in that mirror was the body that had fought the battle while I slept and refused to die before I awoke—the one that had invested itself with strength, guarded my soul, and brought me home to my family. There could not be a more perfect body on Earth.

The scars that cover me are proof of man's capacity for hatred and evil. But these scars speak only of our physical fragility, not the boundless strength in our hearts or the beauty of our collective hope. The battle to rebuild my life has continued for years, but the shadows of the burning towers have been overpowered by the twin beacons of faith and love that guided me forward and led me home. Faith in God, faith in love, and faith in myself have vanquished the emptiness I felt when I thought that I would never see Tyler again or never have a second child. Together, they've formed something so grand, so powerful, that it has raised me up from darkness toward a lightness that still remains.

I take heart in all that I have accomplished in the last decade, but I mourn the loss of a career that had been an integral part of my identity. Wall Street was and is a tough place to work, but I loved the business and the competitive culture. I loved the urgency and the intensity. Perhaps because it in some ways echoed my upbringing, I felt very much at home there.

In that sense, I owe a debt to the rigors of my career. The ruthless competition and the need to prove myself anew every morning helped train me for the job of recovery. I understood that yesterday's results didn't matter if I didn't match or exceed them today. I knew that I had to wake up every morning determined to do my best, resolved that nothing would keep me from achieving the goals I'd set for myself.

Now, having fought and won the battle for my life, I have new goals. Perhaps someday I will return to Wall Street, and I've kept my securities licenses current just in case. But for now I am enjoying being involved in a few business ventures, working with various charitable organizations, and volunteering at Tyler's school. I don't know where the road ahead will take me, but I do know that when I am called by new challenges, I will answer, and once again invest all my energy as I have always done.

My parents, my siblings, and Greg's sisters remain an integral part of our lives, and in December 2010 we joyously celebrated my dad's eightieth birthday with close family. His greatest gift, he told us, was to be surrounded by his four grandsons as we sang "Happy Birthday," and to watch them compete to blow out the candles on his cake.

In November 2002, after publishing his book and spending so much of his time helping me with my recovery, Greg answered Howard's call to join Cantor Fitzgerald and help the firm rebuild. He became a partner in 2006. In 2008, he left to focus on developing innovative technology for digital devices and the financial markets. Sadly, his mother and father, Liz and Bert, who had both been in declining health for several years, died within a month of each other in the fall of 2010. We miss them every day.

Periodically I speak about my experiences, and in May 2003 I gave the commencement address at Columbia University's College of Physicians and Surgeons Programs in Occupational Therapy. I told the graduates that every new patient brings an opportunity to change someone's life, and that if they brought a passion to their treatment that was equal to their skill, they would help their patients find the courage to do their best to heal.

In 2004, Greg and I were honored with the Norman Vincent Peale Award for Positive Thinking by the Blanton-Peale Institute. I took particular pleasure in this award because many years ago I discovered and took to heart a thin blue volume in my parents' home, an original 1952 edition of *The Power of Positive Thinking*. The title of the first chapter is "Believe in Yourself." It's good advice, because choosing to believe in yourself is the single most important choice you can make. It's the choice I made, and it's the choice that allowed me to believe that I would overcome my injury.

In November of 2008, I spoke at the gala of the Koby Mandell Foundation, which was founded by Sherri and Seth Mandell, whose son was murdered by terrorists in May of 2001. Their foundation is dedicated to bridging the isolation that parents and children feel when they have lost a loved one to terrorist violence. We can never countenance the evil that takes a child or any innocent life; we can never surrender to it. In the most meaningful way, the Mandells were driven to action, and toward healing, by the loving image of their son.

All of us have been wounded in some way, whether by violence, disease, or other personal tragedy. But though we can never pretend that we have not been touched by adversity, we can refuse to be held by it. Whether you open your eyes after a single night or seven long weeks, from that moment of awakening your recovery is up to you. The only way forward is to gather your courage and take that lonely first step—the step of commitment, the step that will be remembered for generations.

What will you choose to do, with the time God has given you? Every day you have a choice. Make it count.

It is Father's Day, 2010. Even for June it's unseasonably warm, with temperatures in the nineties and a soaking humidity. The skies are thick with clouds, but they aren't doing much to cool us. Greg, Tyler, and I amble through Central Park, each of us taking turns pushing Jagger in the stroller. A concert is under way at the nearby amphitheater; the sounds of a Latin band sail on the air, and we stop and listen to the infectious Brazilian rhythms and the deep, syncopated bass. Jagger smiles, his mouth broad, his eyes twinkling, and he begins to sway his shoulders to the beat. I'm not surprised, because I already know he has music in his soul. He's our little Night Rider, after all.

We walk south past the Alice in Wonderland statue and the boat pond, ever closer to our destination. Seeing the north entrance, I smile and challenge Ty to a race. With his speed, it is all I can do to stay even with him. We reach the gates damp from the effort and the heat, and then, just as we once did with Tyler, we enter a child's place of dreams.

For Jagger's first Father's Day, Tyler and I have brought Greg to the Central Park Zoo. This time I am not dressed in sun-protective clothing and a broad-brimmed hat; instead, I am wearing a Lilly Pulitzer sea-blue-and-white patterned skirt and a white-collared shirt with short sleeves and two silver buttons at the neck. My scars have diminished, the red rage of healing has receded, and my posture is relaxed. I am easily able to hold Jagger in my arms, even when he squirms. As Greg takes a photograph, I sit next to my little boy, leaning over him and smiling like any proud mother.

We pause in front of the sea lions. Feeding time is starting, and a large crowd is gathering to watch. One sea lion, impatient with waiting, turns up her nose at the trainer and slips into the water. Through the clear glass side of the enclosure we see her swim past us. Moving gracefully and with astonishing speed, she bursts out of the water and onto a rock. Sitting there with a certain insolence, she claps her flippers together.

Jagger looks at the animals intently, full of curiosity and wonder, trying to unravel the mysteries of this new world. Walking into the Children's Zoo, we pass the aviary, and Jagger excitedly points at the birds flitting from branch to branch. Tyler laughs and then bends down to say something to his brother.

The aviary brings to mind a book Tyler read for school this year, a fantasy in which an orphan child—a squirrel—saves a kingdom when he rides home on the back of a swan and conquers evil so that all the animals may safely return. "There is a way home," Tyler wrote of the swans. "They are proud and graceful. They waft through the air soaring through the clouds, drifting; they fly through the mists home."

My voyage home was a journey back to those I loved. As primitive and physical as my struggle was, the spark of recognition and the power to prevail came from a vision of my firstborn son. Then just ten months old, he inspired me to exert my last measure of strength to return to him. Now ten months have become ten years, and the miracle is that I am still here by his side.

I look at my family now and see everything I ever dreamed of, ever hoped for, embodied in these three. I stand between my two sons, the one whom I would not leave, the other whom I vowed to bring home. I know their unscarred innocence is as transient as the flowers in my garden in Sagaponack; only in a children's book can a mother's love provide absolute protection from pain and brutality. Yet I know that I can teach them that even in a world where evil does exist, they are not defeated as long as they have the will to fight and never surrender their dreams.

I reach down to smooth Jagger's hair and am jarred by the intense scarring on my left arm and hand. The flawed skin seems foreign, even though it is very much a part of me. Then I realize that this is the hand I raised to shield my face from the fire, and I smile. My hand, however imperfect, is a living talisman, not of suffering, but of something divine: the power to survive and to heal.

ACKNOWLEDGMENTS

Early one recent afternoon, while Tyler was at school and Jagger napped, I gathered some of Tyler's books and toys and brought them back to his room. As I turned to leave, my eye was drawn to one of his bookshelves and the cracked sculpture of the little yellow lion that he had made while he was still in nursery school. I remembered how proud we were the day he'd brought it home. Now missing a leg, its tail, and one ear, the lion is our story: damaged and imperfect but still standing. Tucked amid his books, photos, and sports trophies, to me it is the greatest prize, the one that represents Tyler himself, the little lion who saved his family from a greater pain than he could ever imagine. My two sons have been my inspiration for writing and for living, and taking every step of my journey in their company is the most precious gift of all.

Thank you my dear Greg for your unerring confidence and commitment and, most of all, for your love. Your faith and belief have never faltered.

Many thanks to my amazing agent, Rob Weisbach, whose positive energy, ongoing enthusiasm, and intellect have been invaluable.

Stephen Rubin at Henry Holt believed in the power of my story, and my editor, John Sterling, brought the passion and commitment to see it through to fruition. I am grateful to everyone else at

Henry Holt for their hard work and their support of this book, including Maggie Richards, Pat Eisemann, Melanie DeNardo, Rick Pracher, and Victoria Haire.

I offer deep gratitude to my beloved friend Barb Burg, whom I met when she was the director of publicity for Bantam Dell and who became a dear friend in the succeeding years while serving on "Retainer for Life." When I finally decided to tell my story in my own words, she was there to help me begin. Our families have now grown up together, and she has always offered her support and her guidance. During the past two years, she found herself in a battle with cancer, and she has conquered it with courage and grace. I am happy beyond words to have her with me, healthy and strong.

I am grateful to my friends, who kept me in their hearts and stayed close to me so that I always felt loved and comfortable in their presence. And I am grateful to all those good people around the world who opened their hearts to me and offered their support in writing or in person. You lifted my spirits during my hardest days, and your good will signals the goodness that lies within all of us.

I can never forget all the friends and colleagues who were killed on September 11, 2001, and as I wrote this book I thought of them constantly and remembered how much they cared for their families. Every breath I share with my family is in part a tribute to their memory, and to the memory of all the innocents who died on that day.

We are all in debt to the men and women of our armed services who have fought the battle both before and after September 11 so that others will not be harmed by terror or tyranny. They have my unending gratitude and my admiration. I send my most profound wishes for a healthy recovery to all those warriors who have been wounded. And to the loved ones of those who have died in the performance of their duty, know that we hold them in the highest respect, and we honor the mission for which they sacrificed their lives.

I send my heartfelt thanks to my Cantor Fitzgerald family, and to Howard and Allison Lutnick and Edie Lutnick, who stood by my family and so many others, and kept us within their embrace.

Thank you to David Groff for your insights and thoughtful suggestions.

I am grateful to my doctors and nurses at the Weill Cornell Burn Center and later the Burke Rehabilitation Hospital, and to the occupational and physical therapists who have done so much to help me rebuild my life, including my occupational therapist Susan Scanga, who has maintained her practice just two blocks from what is now Ground Zero, and my physical therapist Annie Gow. I cannot forget the years of gracious care I received from Pamela Messina at the Center for Specialty Care. Dr. Patrick Fazzari has helped me stay the course on rehabilitation as my needs and challenges have evolved.

I am forever grateful to "Madame Curie"—Kareen Superville—who spent five years as my caregiver, and to Lesma Williams, Louise Alexander, Rehanna Jordan, Minette Lawrence, Marcia Blake, and Sharon Mason, who have helped make my life as normal as possible.

Thank you Joyce Frater, Aneita Reid-Parnell, and now Christine Campbell for taking care of our boys with such love and sensitivity.

I cherish my mother and father and give thanks every day for our relationship, which was reborn in so many ways after September 11. Thanks also to my sister, Gigi, my brother, Scot, and to Laura and Pam and the rest of our families for their constant love and support.

Although a decade has passed since I battled for my life at the Burn Center, the nurses who watched over me every hour for those three months deserve special recognition. Richard Thalman, Lars Updale, and Pauline Lee cared for me during the first, most difficult days, followed by: Jill Abshire, Nicole Alden, Eugene Ambrosio, Alex Baguio, Dawn Battle-Massey, Virginia Bentley, Jennifer Bianchi, Edna Blaise, Zenon Borawski, Andre Cesarski, Nicole Cole, Mervin David, Bobby Dixon, Hantz Dumont, Judith Dziuba, Monica England, Jennifer Estes, Faith Fajarito, Jennifer Forsberg, Marjorie Fortin, Debra Fox, Polly Frank, Sandra Garraway, Michael Geremia, Jonathan Gilbride, Ellen Gilley, Kelly Giudice, Andrew Greenway, Daniel Haughie, Diana Kraus, Jo Kraynick, Gregory Lee, Holly Macklay, Bernadette Maguire, Alison Malarkey, Barbara McGee, Charles Mitchell, Peggy Mitchell, Chanita Montgomery, Oscar Nagrampa, Kenneth Osorio, Arti Panchal, Rafael Portales, Theresa Potocki, Kathleen Pry, Linda Quintiliani, Barbara Ritchwood, Elvira Robateau, Kelly Russell, Meredith Santiago, Sarah Seiler, Roger Tague, Hayes Vargo, Susan Vinge, Tanya Walker, Rhonda Wilson, and Svetlana Zavuroua.

The full crew of occupational and physical therapists who did so much to help me at Weill Cornell include Hope Laznick, Assistant Chief of Physical Therapy, and Robin Silver, Senior Occupational Therapist, as well as Kimberly Broderick, PT; Jennifer Gilbert, OTR; Kimberly Hill, OTA; Rita Ingram, OTR; Tracy Maltz, PT; Maureen Marren, PT; Ivette Mayo, PT; Alyssa Padial, PT; Kerrie Schryver, OTR; Malvina Sher, PT; and Samuel Yohannan, PT.

I believed, and I took that first step. Looking back, I see just how many people were there taking those steps alongside me.

ABOUT THE AUTHOR

LAUREN MANNING is a former managing director and partner at Cantor Fitzgerald. Her story of surviving the 9/11 attacks has been featured on *The Oprah Winfrey Show* and NBC's *Today Show,* in the *New York Times,* and in many other media outlets around the world; CNN recently chose her as one of the most intriguing newsmakers of the past twenty-five years. The recipient of many honors and awards, she lives in New York City with her husband, Greg, and their two sons, Tyler and Jagger.

If you would like to get in touch with Lauren Manning, please email her at lauren@laurenmanning.com.